GROUP TREATMENT IN SOCIAL WORK

AN INTEGRATION OF THEORY AND PRACTICE

SECOND EDITION

GROUP TREATMENT IN SOCIAL WORK

AN INTEGRATION OF THEORY AND PRACTICE

SECOND EDITION

EDCIL WICKHAM

Wilfrid Laurier University

THOMPSON EDUCATIONAL PUBLISHING, INC.

Toronto

        publisher@thompsonbooks.com
        www.thompsonbooks.com
        Telephone: (416) 766-2763
        Fax: (416) 766-0398

Canadian Cataloguing in Publication Data

National Library of Canada Cataloguing in Publication

Wickham, Edcil, 1937-
  Group treatment in social work : an integration of theory and practice / Edcil Wickham. -- 2nd ed.

Includes bibliographical references and index.
ISBN 1-55077-134-5

  1. Social group work--Textbooks. I. Title.
HV45.W53 2003   361.4   C2002-905543-1

Cover illustration: "People and Grailings," Marion Tuu'luq, 1974, Baker Lake. Courtesy of the estate of Marion Tuu'luq.

Marion Tuu'luq was born around 1910, in the Chantrey Inlet / Back River area of Nuvanut, north-west of Hudson Bay. She belonged to a traditional, semi-nomadic group of Inuit who lived, according to the season, in tents or snow houses. When the threat of starvation in the 1960s compelled them to leave the land and move into the settlement of Baker Lake, Tuu'luq acknowledged that she was relieved to have escaped the extremities of her life on the land. But she also felt profound sadness at no longer being able to follow the rhythms of the nomadic life, at no longer experiencing the beauty of life on the very edge of the stark quest for survival. These elements loom large in her work, which is peopled by a profusion of human, animal and spirit figures linked in motifs expressing a unified vision of traditional contemporary Inuit life.

Marion Tuu'luq died in October 2002. The National Gallery of Canada honoured this remarkable artist's vision of the world in a an exhibition of her works from 11 October 2002 to 12 January 2003.

Copy Editing: Elizabeth Phinney
Cover Design: Elan Designs

We acknowledge the support of the Government of Canada through the Book Publishing Industry Development Program for our publishing activities.
We acknowledge the support of the Government of Ontario through the Ontario Media Development Corporation Book Initiative.

Printed in Canada.
1 2 3 4 5 6   07 06 05 04 03

Table of Contents

Preface

There continues to be a great deal of interest in group work as a method of therapeutic treatment. Therapeutic groups are now commonplace in most social and health care settings. However, in spite of the interest and the number of ongoing treatment groups, students and beginning practitioners still experience considerable difficulty when they attempt to integrate the theory and practice of group treatment. The major purpose of this work is to demonstrate ways in which theory informs practice, so that the student or practitioner can develop the ability to integrate theory and practice and to acquire the skills necessary for effective functioning in group treatment. Under discussion are the factors that affect both client and worker, the preparation required before treatment starts and how such treatment may be evaluated.

Section 1 emphasizes the importance of the organizational context and the preparation of both client and worker. A chapter on pre-screening is included with this section. At the end of Section 2, which outlines the stages of group development and the ways in which the worker can use the knowledge of these stages to assist treatment, a chapter on co-leadership is included.

Section 3 presents six case studies that demonstrate how theory informs practice. These case studies have been contributed by: Robert Basso, Ph.D. (Associate Professor, Wilfrid Laurier University); Catherine Martin, M.S.W. (Private Practitioner, Kitchener/Waterloo); Patricia Patterson-Wybrow, M.S.W. (Social Worker at Stonehenge Treatment Centre, Guelph); William Pelech, Ph.D. (Assistant Professor, University of Calgary) and Steven Thibodeau, M.S.W. (Coordinator of the Mental Health Programme, Aakom-Kiyii Health Services, Brocket, Alberta); Christine Tauer-Martin, M.S.W. (Student Services Counsellor, University of Waterloo); and the author.

Introduction

This edition will examine ways in which group work as a method of social work can help clients and practitioners enhance their functioning as human beings. Every group in whatever setting provides the opportunity for personal and collective growth. But for any human activity to be successful, there must be goals, and the degree of success depends on the degree to which the goals are SMART, that is, specific, measurable, achievable, realistic and time-limited.

A vague and generalized goal, such as "helping adolescents behave better," laudable as it may be, is neither specific nor measurable as stated. The most difficult task for the practitioner is to realistically look at this general goal, and the sequential steps necessary to achieve such a goal. Each step on the ladder to success provides the opportunity to set a short-term goal that is SMART. In the process, both client and worker begin to appreciate what is meant by "behaving better." Are there skills to be learned and practiced? For example, are listening skills a part of the picture? From this flows the *activities* that can be designed to develop these skills if they are considered by worker and client to be an essential part of "behaving better."

In every group there will be group goals and personal goals. These goals may be imposed or self-determined, but in any event, activities must be designed to achieve goals whether stated or unstated, personal or collective. The collective goal is often determined by the group's need, but the organization often imposes goals on the group and the worker. Professionals concerned with human development accept the premise that human beings function in relation to a hierarchy of basic needs, and personal goals depend in large measure on where the individual is on this hierarchy of needs.

For example, a Welfare organization may require all of its staff to learn how to set goals in order to work effectively towards setting goals that would reflect the agency's mandate. The ultimate objective of this agency is to ensure that all participants learn to set goals and plan activities and experiences to achieve their stated goals. As the goals of the agency have been imposed on the staff, many staff members have difficulty in accepting the need for them to set personal goals within the framework of the agency's mandate. The staff must be helped to see the need to set SMART goals.

In this edition emphasis will be placed on the importance of goal setting in group work. In group treatment, whether in public or private settings, the practice goals must flow from the organizational context, the worker needs and the client needs. Given this loci of goal positions, the worker has a key role to play in interpreting the organization's goals; setting personal goals within that context and helping the client to establish personal goals. All these goals must be synchronized and work in tandem given the reality that the overriding goal of any group activity is the enhancement of personal growth.

The worker is the "linchpin" in any group work activity. The activities must be designed to help the client identify their needs and articulate SMART goals–short and long term–to meet the identified needs, the steps that must be taken to achieve the stated goals and the methods to be used to evaluate progress towards the achievement of both short- and long-term goals. Implicit in this activity is the need for the worker to identify practice goals that are in keeping with those of the organization and the needs of the client.

The ability of the worker to be an effective linchpin depends to a large extent on a comprehensive knowledge relevant to the subject matter as well as professional competence and varied experience. Practice must be informed by knowledge and experience–the worker must have a firm grasp of human development, group development, group dynamics, group functioning and how these affect practice and be able to observe and evaluate progress towards the achievement of goals.

A new feature of this edition is the inclusion of several case studies that illustrate ways in which theory informs practice and enhances personal experience and professional growth.

PREPARATION FOR GROUP TREATMENT

The worker must be adequately prepared to begin helping in group treatment. In this text the term group treatment refers to any group practice in which the purpose is to initiate or facilitate change in an individual by means of a group process. Change is considered as some shift in attitude, thinking, feeling or functioning in a positive direction. Treatment is seen as a situation in which one or several professional persons help clients to help themselves to examine and to change, where appropriate, their affect, cognition and behavior. In short, treatment is the use of a relationship to help another person to change some attitude, some behavior, some way of thinking or feeling that is presently socially dysfunctional.

The principles used in group treatment can be used to help groups of all types to function effectively through the skillful use of group work processes. The practitioner must have a thorough knowledge of groups and how they function. Only then can this knowledge and skill be applied in any group situation. With group work practice, the practitioner improves both personally and professionally. But the benefits to be derived by all constituents are in direct proportion to the knowledge, skills and experience of the group leader.

Preparation for group treatment involves an evaluation of the organizational auspices under which the treatment program will be conducted. This section will focus on:

- a discussion of the ways in which the organizational context influences and affects the practitioner's approach to his or her work with client groups;
- the resources provided by a given organization to facilitate the treatment process;
- the clients served by the specific organization;
- the worker's personal preparation to initiate the process; and
- the pre-screening and preparation of the client for treatment.

These factors are critically examined as they affect and to some extent determine the worker's performance. Social systems concepts are adapted in order to provide an understanding of the significance of the organizational context in which group treatment is to be conducted.

SECTION 1: CONTENTS

1

The Impact of the Organizational Context on Group Treatment

I t is the responsibility of the worker to understand and take into consideration the auspices under which social group work treatment will be carried out. Social systems concepts provide a framework for studying the dynamics of the organizational context. There are many factors that impinge on an organization and affect not only the functioning of the organization but the functioning of the worker and of the client group. The factors included within the category of organizational context are dynamic and complex. Discussion of these concepts, though by no means comprehensive, will highlight some of the important and relevant features of the context under which group treatment will occur. These concepts are:

- Goals and Objectives
- History
- Traditions
- Funding–Including Fees
- Records
- Hierarchy of Authority
- Communication
- Rules and Regulations
- Culture
- Values
- Attitudes
- Norms
- Codes of Behavior
- Psycho-Social Climate
- Resources
- Societal Interactions

It is the responsibility of the worker to understand these factors and to identify ways of effectively working within the organizational context. The formal system of an organization is usually explicit and easily explained in terms of goals, rules and the "hierarchy of authority" that determines the lines of formal communication. The informal system is less apparent though equally important.

Goals and Objectives

Organizational goals are usually stated clearly in writing and are publicly available. For example, schools are established to educate children and hospitals to treat the sick. If the goals of the organization are not clear it is unlikely that its program goals and objectives will be clear to the workers or clients. The goal of a given social agency may be to improve the social functioning of a particular group in a given catchment area. Another agency may be set up to aid specific groups during times of crisis or stress. The clearer the goals of the organization, the easier it is for the worker to select clients to be served by that organization and for clients to select the organization through which they hope to gain the service needed. In addition, when the goals are clear other organizations are more likely to refer clients appropriately. An organization having clearly defined goals can also minimize the conflict between the expectations that workers and clients might have and what the agency is realistically able to offer.

History

The history of an organization is a critical variable that the worker needs to understand and take into consideration when planning treatment. The history encompasses all the traditions, decisions and formal and informal practices that have developed in the organization from its beginning to the present.

Without a good knowledge of the history of the organization, a worker may find that, in an effort to develop a treatment group, the goals, strategies, resources and even the composition of the group may be contrary to the many traditional approaches of the organization and therefore invite "frustration"–frustration by supervisors, administrators and even maintenance staff. The opposite is also true. The worker who has done his or her homework is aware of the organization's values, traditions and statutes and is then able to use these to the benefit of the client group.

In order to understand the organizational context the worker must look critically at the history of the organization and see how it influences or affects the role and function of the worker who is part of the system. Each organization is developed to meet a particular need within the community it serves. An organization may traditionally develop a service for a particular client group, such as all persons who are going through separation and divorce or persons who are addicted to alcohol or drugs. It may have developed ways of providing that service either through groups or with individuals. There may be specific directions for workers to function in particular ways and an indication of how problems and issues have been resolved over time.

If such a system exists, then the worker cannot ignore it. To attempt to offer service to clients who have not been traditionally served by that organization would lead to conflict that may be difficult to resolve. Moreover, if the organization has always failed to provide adequate resources there is no reason to believe that there would be a significant increase in resources for a new group. Hence, both the client and the worker are affected by the values, philosophy and goals of the organization.

Generally, all this information may be found in the records of the organization or can be ascertained by interviewing key persons in the organization. Organizations are creatures of their history and their future is in large measure determined by that history.

Traditions

The history of an organization usually indicates the traditions that have developed within that organization. Social agencies, hospitals, institutional and industrial settings that provide social treatment all evolve within the context of the given culture. It is reasonable to expect then that these organizations would reflect some of the cultural aspects of the larger society of which they are a part. For example, if there is a cultural norm about the way that people discuss their personal situation, then the organization is likely to build in structures that support such a norm.

For example, some ethnic groups find it difficult to discuss financial problems in a group situation; it is simply not done. The organization would therefore offer treatment services with that cultural orientation in mind. It would veto group treatment for credit counseling and favor individual treatment. The worker who is not mindful of the impact of the culture on the organization may be working at cross-purposes with the organization and the client group.

Funding: Including Fees

The history of the organization includes information on how that organization has been funded in the past and, by implication, the prospects for future funding. The adage "he who pays the piper calls the tune" is particularly valid here. The funding source will often spell out specific criteria, restrictions and guidelines for the receipt of its funds. These requirements would, of necessity, significantly influence the ability of an organization to deliver certain types of treatment services.

The manner in which an organization has used its resources to meet the needs of past clients gives the worker some indication of the way it is likely to react and respond to a new group treatment program. If, traditionally, an organization has given priority to serving the treatment needs of a specific age range of clients, there may be reasons, real or imaginary, for not encouraging a worker to serve a different age group. For example, an organization may not have the resources or the personnel for establishing teen-age groups if historically it has served pre-schoolers.

Another aspect of funding that may influence the delivery and use of treatment services may be whether the client is expected to subsidize or even pay in full for the services offered. A willingness to pay for services may be seen as an indication that the client values the service and the extent to which the client is motivated to change. Thus, the payment of fees could be seen by some organizations as a valuable tool in the treatment process.

Funding may also determine, for both client and worker, the number and length of the sessions the organization deems appropriate for the completion of the treatment tasks.

Records

The limits of funding may also influence the extent and general adequacy of the records kept by the organization. Records are kept for two purposes. First, to ensure that there is a permanent record of the client's goals, objectives and treatment. These are documented to ensure continuity and avoid duplication in the event that it is not possible for the worker to continue working with the group. Secondly, records allow workers to follow not only the progress of the client toward personal goals but also the goals and general direction of the group. The only practical way of maintaining continuity for the individual client and the worker is through adequate records.

All organizations determine what they want recorded and how the information they collect will be recorded. The organization also determines whether the recordings will be treated confidentially or not. Again, the patterns established by the organization are of supreme importance and must be understood. Confidentiality is an important issue that must be addressed by the organization and the worker. It is necessary for the worker to know how records are treated in the particular organization. The worker must be able to inform the client of what the policies are on recording, the merit of such recording and how it will assist them in achieving their goals and objectives. If the worker is in disagreement with the stated policy of the organization he or she has a responsibility to discuss such disagreements with persons in authority within the organization and not with the client, since this may adversely affect the treatment process. The keeping of records is part of the larger system of communication within the organization.

Hierarchy of Authority

A hierarchy is established within the organization and becomes a formal system that clearly defines lines of communication and authority. A school system provides a clear example of this hierarchy. The school principal is in charge of the school and teachers are accountable to the principal who is in turn accountable to a defined person of authority within the Board of Education.

There are many facets to the hierarchical aspect of an organization's structure. Authority, in most organizations, is vested in policy-making groups with an executive officer who administers the policies and staff who carry out the policies. Between the Chief Executive Officer and the line staff there may be supervisors who significantly influence the delivery of treatment services. If the hierarchy is clear to the worker he or she will readily understand who to turn to for administrative direction. On the other hand, if it is unclear who decides what within the organization then it would be difficult to organize and implement the treatment process. Of equal importance is the clients' perception of the hierarchy of authority within the organization. A clear understanding of the policy-making and administrative functions within the organization will lead to clarity of purpose for the treatment sequence for both worker and client.

Communication

Closely linked with the hierarchy of authority is the flow of formal communication. Information flows through persons in an organization vertically and horizontally. Since information must flow through people, it is possible for the flow to be blocked, diverted or interrupted by individuals at any level in the organization for any number of reasons.

The flow of information through formal channels may not always provide vital information about a client quickly enough to be of value to the worker in setting up the group treatment process. Furthermore, information, even misinformation, about some aspect of the organization's functioning can be inadvertently communicated, creating anxiety and having a negative impact on group functioning.

The systems or methods of both formal and informal communication within the organization must be examined in order to understand how persons relate to each other. If information is not passed on, if it is misconstrued or misinterpreted, then services may be inadequate. If there are good communication networks among workers and staff at all levels, the client is likely to benefit from improved communication because there is a higher probability that the client's needs will be adequately communicated.

Before initiating a treatment group, and during the group sessions, the worker should prepare adequate records on the group process and on the clients who form the group. Not to have the information that an individual may have been disruptive in all groups to date may be to set up the machinery to sabotage effective group treatment for others.

It is easy to ignore the informal communication networks within and between organizations. The informal systems may pass on information about the clients that may interfere with the achievement of treatment goals. These networks may prejudice the worker in relation to a specific client. The worker may function on hearsay rather than on observed or documented behavior.

Rules and Regulations

Rules are established in an organization to modify behavior toward the achievement of the stated goals. Rules and regulations are made by the policy makers for the smooth functioning of all aspects of the organization. One such aspect is the kind of treatment processes that will be initiated and developed by workers for clients. The organization may determine the basis for serving a particular client group. If this is not understood by the worker then there may be some unnecessary conflict between the worker and other members of the organization. Yet, this is not to suggest that the worker should not try to have rules and regulations changed on behalf of the client if such a change is considered beneficial to the client. The climate within an organization influences the codifying and implementation of the rules and regulations that govern its functioning. Rules and regulations, to a large extent, determine how the organization will relate to other organizations, to staff within the organization, to clients and the general public.

The clarity of the rules and regulations, their perceived significance and the ease with which they can be followed, will impinge on the worker and affect his or her ability to engage in a group treatment process. The rules and regulations affect the relationship between the worker and the supervisor and between the worker and the clients. The worker should make every effort to understand how these rules and regulations affect one's ability to begin a new group in the organization, for example, how pre- screening will be done or the time frame for the number and length of group treatment sessions. There may be rules governing the use of the physical plant, especially as these relate to clients that could create or mitigate against a healthy, accepting and warm working environment.

Culture

Organizations develop a culture that encompasses customs and traditions, values, attitudes and beliefs. Culture develops from the pattern of relationships and interactions among people. These patterns become the commonly accepted ways of coping with typical situations; they become norms. For example, family service agencies have different cultures affected by styles of leadership, communication patterns and traditions. A worker who behaves in a way that does not conform to the agency's expectations will often incur disapproval and censure. In an agency that prides itself on strict adherence to client confidentiality, the worker who discusses his or her clients with the media, however general and non-specific such discussion may be, may still be considered by the agency and peers to have breached confidentiality.

Values

The ideals, traditions and norms of an organization are shaped by values. Values are preferred ways of behaving and thinking. An organization's values can often be determined by perusing its mission statement and its stated goals and objectives.

The values held within an organization are critical to the group treatment process. If an organization considers group treatment to be the preferred method of meeting the needs of its clients, then one can expect that resources will be made available to its workers and clients to establish group treatment programs. If, on the other hand, the organization is committed to another method of service delivery, the worker may find it very difficult to convince the decision makers in the organization to make adequate resources available for group treatment.

It is difficult to identify the values within a social system, except as they are seen as preferred ways of behaving. Here we would mean preferred ways of providing service to clients. The preferred way, in a given agency, may be through the individual or the family modality. If this is the preferred way of offering service it is reasonable to expect that an attempt by a worker to provide services in a group mode would not be supported. This lack of support could lead to frustration and the denial of service to clients who may need such service at a very critical time in their development.

Attitudes

Attitudes reflect a person's values and in large measure determine that person's actions. When the values of an organization are incompatible with individual values, tension and conflicts result. As an example, an agency may see itself as committed to providing group work services to clients. How these services are provided will be influenced by the preferences of the coordinator of the program and ultimately by the workers actually providing the service who may collectively or simply prefer another modality.

Very closely aligned to norms, values and traditions are the attitudes and beliefs of the persons who make up the social system. There may be within a social agency the belief that only a specific type of treatment modality is valuable or useful to a particular group of clients. If this attitude is held by key persons in the agency, it will affect the support given to a worker who wants to set up a treatment group within that agency. On the other hand, if attitudes and beliefs are supportive of the group treatment process, then one may expect that any attempt to set up a treatment group would be encouraged.

Norms

Norms are shaped by values, attitudes and traditions. They are commonly understood and accepted standards of behavior. For example, an organization may have developed a dress code for all front-line workers indicating that, when interacting with clients in the office, ultra-casual attire is not acceptable. The new worker who arrives in jeans quickly gets the message and soon realizes that this attire is unacceptable even though there may be no verbal comment or reprimand.

Norms, within a social system's context, are the ways of doing things that have been accepted by all members of that particular system. The norms of an organization would influence the delivery of services. If the services offered are not compatible with the norms of the organization there will be overt and covert actions to sabotage the group treatment process. The worker must be aware of and understand the dynamics of the situation in which he or she plans to offer services and the ways in which these dynamics affect the development of group treatment.

Codes of Behavior

Over time all social systems develop ways of behaving toward external systems and internally in relation to the units or members that make up the organization. Such patterns of behavior places powerful expectations on its members to behave in particular ways in relation to the functions they perform. In the organizational context, there are expectations for all levels of the organization to perform their tasks and duties in particular ways, for example, responding to requests for information about the organization and its programs. This is usually determined by tradition and in keeping with community standards. Through these practices roles become codified and persons joining the organization are expected to follow these practices. Clients, too, are expected to conform to specific codes of behavior. For example, in some organizations, clients are expected to complete certain forms before service is offered.

Psycho-Social Climate

The psycho-social climate of an organization is an amalgam of its history, traditions, values, norms, rules and regulations and the ways in which the members of the organization perceive, accept and adhere to all of the above. The climate generated by an organization may be democratic, autocratic, laissez-faire or combinations of these. In democratic organizations there is active participation in decision making. In some organizations, clients are involved in the decision-making process and are, therefore, likely to feel that their opinions matter.

On the other hand, in an organization that is autocratic or that projects such an image, clients may withdraw from any decision making because they perceive themselves as being ignored by the policy makers, administrators and workers. Such an organization tells the client "we know what's good for the organization and for you." Clients have no option in determining how they define their problems or how they might attempt to solve them. In the laissez-faire climate, the client may get the impression that the organization is disorganized and has nothing to offer and may discontinue using the service.

Less tangible, but related to the organization's climate may be the messages, verbal and non-verbal, that clients receive from the organization. These messages may tell the clients that the building is more important than they are; that it is not really for the use of people. Such an atmosphere may give the clients the feeling that they are not welcome. Another climate may suggest to the clients that the client is wanted, with the concurrent message that the building and things around the building are less important to the organization than is the client. The psycho-social environment of an organization can make it either easy or difficult for clients to engage fully in the treatment process.

Resources

Although group treatment programs can be carried on with limited resources, such programs can be enhanced and treatment accelerated with the provision of adequate resources. For example, if sessions can be video taped and replayed for member and leader evaluation, insights may be more readily grasped than if worker and client were solely dependent on memory. Often, the physical plant can be arranged in ways conducive to group learning. For example, the spatial arrangement of the members, the lighting, the color, and the temperature of the room all affect ambience, interaction and the psychological well-being of the group. A room that is well lit bright and airy contributes to the psychological well-being of the group. If the organization is committed to group work as a treatment modality it is more likely to provide the resources that the worker considers necessary for the enhancement of treatment. The resources that the agency makes available to the worker may include support staff, equipment, volunteer personnel, adequate space and release time in order to facilitate group treatment.

Societal Interactions

All social systems interact with the larger society. Organizations interact with other social agencies and systems. The worker must be mindful of the potential impact of other organizations and systems on practice. A few that are noteworthy are the family, religious organizations, political systems, and other organizations. These systems and many others may determine the type of service an organization is able to provide for its clients.

Many organizations refer their clients to other organizations to work on treatment issues. The relationship that develops between two organizations is critical to the treatment process. Tensions can arise between organizations and it is incumbent upon each and all of them to establish clear lines of communication and have clear messages transmitted. Hopefully, there will be little or no hint of competition among agencies either for clients or to provide services for the clients. The interdependence of organizations should not be overlooked. There may be a need for an organization offering treatment to request resources from other organizations. For example, access to recreational facilities may be required for a children's group. If there is not a good working relationship or good communication between the organizations, then there will be problems the children's treatment may not be facilitated.

The interactions with the society as a whole affect, or indeed partly determine, the social, psychological and emotional climate of an organization. As the meteorological climate is affected by such factors as wind, rain, sun, barometric pressure, land mass and bodies of water, so too is the climate of an organization affected by the attitudes of the dominant professional group, by inter-personal rivalries, by the decision-making process and by the many and varied factors that interact with each other and the organization to create its own unique psychological climate. Each organization through the interactions of its personnel, the design of the physical plant, even the color schemes in the plant, creates its own distinctive climate or psycho-social environment. These features, because of their complexity, must be given careful consideration as treatment is planned and developed.

The following case material highlights most if not all of the variables that affect a worker's functioning in an organizational context.

Mr. Andrews, a social worker with five years experience, was hired by a school board and assigned to provide services to five public schools with classes from kindergarten to grade seven. As a first step in learning about the school system he met with the social worker he would be replacing. He found that she served as an attendance counselor; a role he was not interested in continuing. His experience included therapeutic work with children who were underachieving in school due to behavioral problems and social adjustment difficulties. He had achieved considerable success using group treatment programs. He hoped to offer similar services in the school system.

After meeting with Ms. Robinson, the social worker he was replacing, he realized he would have to move slowly and sensitively to change the traditional social work roles that had been established. Following her suggestion, he met with the school principal she considered most knowledgeable about social and emotional problems.

Mr. Dorchester, the school principal, greeted Mr. Andrews warmly and seemed interested in the possibilities for expanding the range of social work services in the school. However, he was hesitant to proceed without discussion with the Board officials and other principals. He suggested Mr. Andrews meet with the other principals and agreed to set up the meeting.

Two weeks later the meeting was held with the five principals and a board representative. The lines of authority and the formal system were clear. Mr. Andrews made a presentation suggesting a broader range of social work services than traditionally offered by Ms. Robinson and shared his experience in direct work with children and families. He was careful to observe any interest or support from members of the group. Two principals stated strongly they did not need further services and could manage any problems except truancy on their own. They had not found social workers very helpful in the past. Two others showed some tentative interest and said they would call Mr. Andrews if problems arose. The board representative agreed to support a small trial program for underachieving children if the principals wished to try it. Mr. Dorchester was interested enough to meet with Mr. Andrews to discuss the idea further.

It was clear to Mr. Andrews that the best hope for expanding services was through Mr. Dorchester and he decided to concentrate his efforts in Mr. Dorchester's school initially.

Two weeks later he met again with Mr. Dorchester and they discussed the characteristics of the area served by the school and the problems the teachers encountered in the classrooms. Mr. Andrews presented possible ways he might help, making sure he acknowledged that any plan would be possible only if Mr. Dorchester approved. He quickly realized that Mr. Dorchester needed to demonstrate that he was in charge of his school and any threat to his authority would close the door to further discussions.

Although there was no commitment to expanding services Mr. Dorchester did agree that Mr. Andrews could attend a staff meeting with the teachers and present his ideas for providing counseling services.

Three weeks later, Mr. Andrews attended the staff meeting and shared his experiences with similar children and how he had worked to help them. Four teachers were able to identify with the problems he described and began to discuss the students that presented problems for them. Mr. Andrews encouraged discussion of ways they coped with the children who were disruptive or failed to participate in class. As they talked, the informal system was revealed: and the informal leaders were evident. Mr. Andrews supported their efforts to help the children and their dedication to teaching. Their trust and respect for Mr. Dorchester was also evident. During the meeting a beginning relationship between Mr. Andrews and the teachers was established and a willingness to talk to him was expressed. It was also clear he was still an outsider in this school system.

During the next two months Mr. Andrews met informally with the teachers on an individual basis. He made special efforts to talk to two teachers who were the leaders in the informal system. One of them invited him to sit in on a class to observe the children who were disruptive. There were four boys, nine to eleven years of age, who were restless, unable to pay attention and socially rejected by most other students. Mr. Andrews admired how well the teacher coped with them for five hours each day. It was evident that this teacher was an excellent, caring teacher and the principal deliberately assigned difficult-to-handle children to her. It was evident also that she was under considerable stress trying to cope with the problem behaviors and also meet the needs of the other children.

As Mr. Andrews and the teacher talked, a mutual respect developed and she was willing to support a trial project using Mr. Andrew's group approach to help the four boys identified in the classroom.

Mr. Andrews and the teacher met with Mr. Dorchester and the teacher's growing respect for Mr. Andrews went a long way in convincing Mr. Dorchester to try a group treatment approach. The goal of the group was to improve their academic performance by increasing their self-esteem, improving their social skills and increasing their level of social and emotional maturity.

Mr. Dorchester was concerned about parental approval for the program and it was agreed that the parents needed to be involved. Fortunately, parental involvement in the school program, including an active Parent-Teacher Association was a tradition in Mr. Dorchester's school, so including parents was not a major obstacle. Mr. Dorchester, as principal in charge of the school, invited the parents of the children to be included in the group to a meeting to discuss the plan and request their approval.

During the next two weeks, six boys, nine to eleven years of age from two classes, were identified as appropriate for group treatment.

Two weeks later a parents' meeting was held with Mr. Dorchester as chair. All the parents supported the group if it was going to benefit the children. Two parents expressed disappointment in their children's poor academic performances. Others worried about their children's lack of friends. Mr. Andrews recognized that serious family stresses existed in two families and pressure on the children to excel was clear in two others. He suggested that the parents meet once a month to give and receive feedback during the pilot project. Mr. Andrews also hoped to encourage the parents to modify the pressure they placed on the children, give them more positive feedback and in two instances, possibly refer them for help with their many problems.

Mr. Andrews recognized that in spite of encouraging progress, he was still on trial in this school and how he continued to work with the formal and informal systems would influence the success or failure of the program. The four other schools were observing with detached interest not only the program but the response of school board officials.

Five months after the first discussion with Mr. Dorchester, the first group meeting was held.

Even though the first group session was five months in coming, there seemed to be a good foundation for the group treatment process to begin.

Summary

An examination of the various components of an organization as a social system shows how these components affect the worker. The worker, in this context, was seen as an agent of change. He or she does not necessarily attempt to change the social system but strives to use the system to help clients move toward the achievement of the goals which were established by the client within the treatment group. The question to be addressed, then, is: how does each aspect of the agency, institution or organization affect the worker and his work with client groups?

Each social system has a unique life of its own yet depends on other systems for survival. This is true of agencies, institutions, and indeed all organizations. The worker is part of this unique social entity, which connects up with other social entities in the society of which we are all a part.

In each social system there are units that are interdependent even though they may at times function independently. In an organization, individuals, which would include staff at all levels, function interdependently and at times independently, but they are all necessary to the survival of the organization. If a worker is unaware of the interdependence that exists between himself or herself and others in the organization that worker may fail to recognize or pay attention to the influence of other persons in the organization upon him or her. This failure can impede the ability to function competently with co-workers and clients. The same would be true of a worker who tries to function independently of other members of a team or an organization, especially when establishing treatment groups. The worker who fails to recognize the interrelationship of persons in their varying roles within the organization is unable to appreciate the powerful effect that this can have on the services offered to clients. This lack of awareness may mean that the worker does not utilize available resources to enhance the group treatment process.

Social systems theory provides a useful framework for looking at organizational structure and how it affects the worker, the client and group treatment. It allows us to examine in an orderly fashion the various aspects of an organization and their impact on the worker and clients.

The goals and objectives of the organization are important and should be emphasized. If these are clearly stated then it seems that the worker is only limited by the kind of treatment modality accepted by the organization to be used with the particular client group. The client group should be made aware of the organization's purpose and how their particular group will be affected by that purpose. One such objective is the social change of the individual in a group context in which the worker is seen as a change agent with the support and authority of the organization. Each aspect of the organization and its functioning affects the worker and he in turn affects the client and the group treatment process. It would be a useful exercise for the reader to identify the relevant variables within his or her own organization and how they affect, or might have affected, his or her functioning.

QUESTIONS FOR CONSIDERATION

In planning a group treatment program, consider the following:

1. How congruent are your goals for the group with those of the organization?

2. What has been the history and tradition of group services within the organization?

3. What resources and support services will be required and are these available? If not available, what are the alternatives?

4. How would you handle issues of confidentiality in relation to your group?

5. Who makes the decisions about group services to clients?

6. What information does the organization need from you, the worker, in order to evaluate your proposals for group treatment services?

7. What are the best ways of providing this information, formally and informally?

8. How will others in the organization be affected by your treatment group?

9. Who needs to be involved in the planning of the group treatment program within and outside the organization? How do you plan to do this? How do you plan to gain their cooperation and support?

2

Worker Preparation for Group Treatment

The worker's purpose for the group treatment encounter is affected by a number of factors. The most important of these includes:

- the impact of the organization on the worker;
- the worker's knowledge base;
- the worker's experiential background, especially with clients and groups; and
- the composition of the specific client group.

To ignore any of these factors is to set the stage for the worker to miscue on some of the most critical dynamics of the treatment process.

As part of the preparation for the first meeting, the worker needs to be clear about his or her purpose or goals. When thinking of the group treatment process, some purpose is implicit–the overall purpose of bringing individuals together in a group is for treatment. Treatment in this context means helping individuals feel, think, and behave more effectively in their social interactions.

Klein (1972), in his book *Effective Group Work*, suggests that there are the following specific purposes that he considers appropriate for treatment groups:

(1) to enhance self-image;

(2) to share anxieties and test judgments;

(3) to learn to communicate;

(4) to learn to relate to others;

(5) for catharsis;

(6) to resolve the conflict between wish and fear by reducing fear;

(7) to externalize suppressed feelings;

(8) to improve reality testing;

(9) to aid in socialization;

(10) to provide a treatment experience that would help the client to develop a sense of identity; and

(11) to motivate for therapy.

If the specific purpose for which the group is established is unclear there is likely to be confusion, not only for the worker but for the members of the group as well.

Impact of the Organization on the Worker's Purpose

As part of establishing treatment goals, the worker must understand the impact of the organization's goals, how these goals affect the interpretation of the task's execution and performance. All organizations develop a sense of mission in relation to the clients they purport to serve. For example, a Children's Services Center would be likely to have the purpose of serving children in need. However, to pursue this goal effectively it may be necessary to offer programs to parents. Such programs may be designed to improve or enhance parenting skills and abilities in order to help the child improve his or her social functioning and it would be imperative to treat the parents to improve their parenting skills. A worker assigned to a parent's group in such an organization would be likely to have his or her purpose predetermined. The purpose would be to enhance the parenting skills of the parents, so that they are better able to meet the developmental needs of their children.

After taking into account the organization's goals the worker can now begin to establish goals for group programs for the parents and for the children. The worker's goals for the groups could be: (a) that the clients improve their self-image; (b) learn to express emotions in socially acceptable ways; and ©) learn to use their energies in constructive ways. It would be a mistake to establish goals for the group aimed at improving educational performance. Such a goal may be contrary to the goals of the organization. Furthermore, the organization may not have the resources to work for the achievement of educational goals. Certain resources are necessary if the worker is to teach children to use their energies in constructive ways. Facilities for physical activity in a gym, craft shop or outdoors would need to be provided or be made accessible. If the resources required by the worker are not provided by the organization through its administrators the worker may have to change or modify the treatment goals. Communication of the projected specific needs of the group must be made by the worker to the organization. Alternatives must be explored and presented for consideration.

Support through the Supervisory Process

An organization may indicate to its workers that it is supportive of their group treatment activities by providing adequate supervision and consultation. As the worker articulates his or her purposes for the group member and the group, the supervisor may indicate how the organization can provide the necessary resources, or assist the worker in acquiring such resources through other organizations in the community.

The organization may also indicate support by recognizing that it does not have the internal expertise to adequately assist workers with the planned group treatment programs and by providing consultation from another organization or competent professional.

Impact of Organizational Climate

The organization may provide a stimulating and exciting environment in which the worker can work toward the achievement of purposes and goals, communicate the need for specific resources, for adequate supervision and share any problems or concerns that arise. The converse is also possible and then the worker is faced with the challenge of devising ways and means of achieving the treatment goals of the group within the constraints of the organization. For example, an organization that is overly critical of a worker's initiative, and constantly reminds the worker of his or her failings and shortcomings, can expect that the ability of the worker to set appropriate treatment goals will be negatively affected.

Impact of the Knowledge Base on the Worker's Purpose

Basic to the development of the worker's goals and purposes for group treatment is an understanding of specific areas of theory. The worker should understand:

- normal behavior that would include the stages of human development;
- the stages of group development;
- the goal-setting process; and
- social systems concepts.

In attempting to set realistic goals for a proposed client group that has been involved in acts of vandalism, the worker would need to take into consideration the age of the clients as well as their stage of intellectual, physical, emotional and social development. In order to do this, the worker must be aware of what is normal. Goals achievable by normal sixteen-year-olds would be inappropriate for eight-year-olds and probably beyond the reach of handicapped sixteen-year-olds, depending on whether the handicap were social, physical, intellectual or emotional.

Stages of Group Development

All groups begin as a collection of individuals. Before the collection of individuals can be considered a group it must go through recognizable stages of development. These stages are sequential but not discrete as progression from one stage to another is dependent on the successful completion of specific tasks related to the preceding stage. In a treatment group, worker and clients must agree on a common purpose. As the individuals meet to pursue this common purpose, a new social unit is created and this newly created social system becomes a treatment group largely dependent on the purpose.

The stages of group development are labeled differently by such authors as Corey and Corey (1982); Dimock (1976) and Garland, Jones and Kolodny (1965) to mention a few. But the major characteristics identified are remarkably similar. The stages as postulated by Garland, Jones and Kolodny (1965) afford the beginning practitioner definitions specific enough to be of great assistance in understanding the progression of the stages and what occurs during each stage. These stages in order of progression are:

- Pre-affiliation
- Power and Control
- Intimacy
- Differentiation
- Separation

It is difficult for a group to progress to the stage of intimacy without completing most of the tasks related to power and control and pre-affiliation. This is not to imply that the stages of group development do not re-occur throughout the life of the group or are not seen in some form during each session.

The worker must be aware of the stages of group development and their progression in order to plan and develop achievable and realistic goals and objectives for a group and to assess, evaluate and predict some of the changes that are likely to occur in the group. For example, having decided to use the group treatment model with adolescents who have been involved in acts of vandalism, the long-term goal would be to help group members to change their anti-social behavior to socially acceptable behavior. Recognizing that in becoming a group these individuals will change in specific ways, the worker must be able to use his knowledge of the stages of group development as a means of achieving the ultimate goal. If the worker fails to use this knowledge there will be major obstacles and frustrations that will hinder the achievement of the group's goals.

During the pre-affiliation stage, adolescents will be tentative in reaching out to each other and to the worker. The worker should be aware of this tendency and should seek to develop an atmosphere in which teenagers feel safe, but not necessarily comfortable, as they reach out. If, on the other hand, this tentativeness is perceived by the worker as the beginning of the stage of intimacy and he or she attempts to foster a level of intimacy, this could lead to disastrous consequences for the group. Group members are not ready for a higher level of collective functioning at the beginning of the group experience.

The group treatment process is designed with two primary foci, namely to help individuals as members of the group to learn how to set goals in relation to their needs, basic or hierarchical; and secondly, to assist members of the group to acquire the necessary skills to rank their goals and work towards achieving their clearly stated goals.

Having indicators that would show how success in achieving goals will be measured gives the practitioner strong direction regarding the types of activities the group should be engaged in to achieve positive results. In order to achieve goals, the practitioner must be able to set realistic goal (SMART goals): plan and implement activities that are designed to achieve the stated goals, whether short or long term; and also be able to evaluate progress towards the achievement of the goal and if necessary, adapt or modify the activities and strategies. Much of the goal-setting process is in effect a problem-solving process.

The Problem-Solving Process

A major objective of the group treatment process is to help the individuals as members of the group to acquire problem-solving skills that will enable them to take control of their lives. To achieve this the worker must know and demonstrate competence in the use of the problem-solving techniques. This means that the worker must, during treatment, be able to assist the group to:

- Identify the problems, issues or concerns and rank them;
- Collect data on the problems, issues or concerns;
- Critically analyze the data;
- Examine the options, including the available resources;
- Select the most appropriate options and attendant consequences and rank them;

- Decide on the options to be explored;
- Choose and implement an option; and
- Devise procedures for evaluation and feedback in relation to the choice of option.

It is a well known axiom that people learn by doing. Hence, it is imperative that in order to teach teenagers to change their delinquent behavior the worker must be able to take the group through the problem-solving sequence. As the group goes through this sequence, members gain knowledge and understanding of a method that they can use to solve this and other problems in their lives.

This approach is a method of dealing with problems that must be an integral and an on-going strategy used by the worker throughout the treatment experience. In working with the delinquent teenager, at the beginning session when the major objective is to provide a safe environment, the problem-solving strategy can be employed. The worker, in an effort to identify the problem, can ask the members to write down their perceptions and feelings regarding the purpose for being there. This information could be collected anonymously and shared with the group using a discussion format. In this way the problem-solving process would have been initiated with the direct involvement of all the members.

Social Systems Concept

A system is made up of units that interact with each other for the effective functioning of the whole. Each unit has a clearly designated function, but is dependent on other units within the system for effective functioning. To explain the social systems concept, examples will be given from sociological characteristics of the nuclear family. In a social system such as the nuclear family, with units of mother, father and children, roles are often clearly defined and this allows the individual to be clear about their expected role. When one unit fails to perform the generally accepted and designated role the whole system is affected and can become dysfunctional. As an example, in a family when one parent, because of illness, is unable to perform his or her designated role, disequilibrium is created in the family. Singly or collectively the other members are forced to adjust and, at times, assume the neglected role in addition to their designated roles in an effort to compensate for the malfunctioning unit.

Likewise, as the group develops it becomes a social system; it does not start with clearly defined roles. Such roles evolve as the group develops. Some of these roles are leader, follower, scapegoat, clarifier, facilitator, initiator, and are crucial to the development of the group. As members play out their various roles, they demonstrate, to a large extent, the problems and issues that have made treatment necessary. As the group moves through its stages of development, the worker is able to assess whether or not the role a particular member is portraying is appropriate. Inappropriate roles in the group are likely to indicate inappropriate roles in the member's social and personal function. The worker must recognize and be prepared to work with the group as roles develop. Hence a purpose for the treatment session is to facilitate the development of the group as a social system. If the individuals remain as separate, disparate units, this will work against the achievement of the group's goals and the worker may be inclined to conduct one-to-one counseling in a group context.

The Impact of the Worker's Past Experiences on Purpose

Past experience affects present functioning. A worker's experiences, including interactions with clients, other professionals and the general public, as well as interactions at a personal level, all affect at the conscious and sub-conscious level, his or her way of functioning. The individual who may have been exposed to abuse or neglect will bring a set of expectations to a treatment situation that would be very different from those of a person who has been reared in a sheltered and caring environment.

The worker who has had previous experience only with physically handicapped young people is not necessarily prepared to cope with emotionally handicapped young people. A worker who has experienced difficulty setting up group treatment programs is likely to approach a new treatment situation with the over-riding goal of personal success. This could work against the achievement of the group's goals and, for example, such a worker may be driven to take the initiative for resolving the clients' problems rather than taking the clients through the problem-solving process because personal success might seem less assured through the latter approach. Then, too, the worker who has had personal or vicarious experience of delinquent behavior could over-identify with the problems and issues faced by a group of delinquents, and be less effective in leading the group through its problem-solving process.

The worker who is aware of these possibilities, who has a sound knowledge base and has had successful experiences with groups of clients using the problem-solving approach will be more likely to use such experiences to enhance the group treatment encounter. The effective worker will consciously draw on past experiences when developing some of the goals and purposes of the treatment group. The goals of the worker are likely to be achievable and realistic when they are based on sound theoretical principles and concepts that have been adapted or corroborated by successful experience.

The Impact of the Specific Client Group on the Worker's Purpose

Every group is different. Differences may be in age, educational background, socio-economic status, psycho-social functioning, ethnic background, physical abilities and capacities and mixtures of the above. For example, a group may be focused on weight loss as its unifying characteristic but may be composed of persons from varying socio-economic levels, differing age groups and educational backgrounds.

The worker who is planning a treatment group must be aware of and take into consideration the attributes of the client group and the primary problem that has brought the group together. For example, a group of clients may be brought together to work with a common problem such as obesity. Members of the group may have various motivations for being in such a group (medical, psychological and social), and they may vary widely in age from eighteen to seventy years. If the worker has as a major goal the enhancement of self image, he or she may find that some members of the group may react negatively to the treatment process because they perceive their problems as medical rather than psycho-social. Obviously the worker should recognize that, depending on the composition of the client group there may need to be several purposes or several groups.

Summary

Clearly stated goals and objectives are to a large extent dependent on the worker's theoretical knowledge and experience. A clear sense of purpose emerges when the worker is competent and knowledgeable about the theories and constructs around:
- the factors that affect personality development;
- the dynamics of group functioning and development;
- the group as a social system; and
- the systems that impact on the group.

In addition to the above, the worker's goals for the group are influenced by an understanding of the impact of the organization under whose auspices group treatment is offered. Moreover, the particular issues and concerns of the client group to be served will influence the development of the worker's treatment goals for individual members and the group.

Each worker has a personal philosophy about helping those in need. This philosophy needs to be clarified by the worker who must objectively consider how this influences the goals for the group. It is conceivable that a worker's commitment to help could be self-serving. A worker may get gratification out of helping for the sake of helping, for the boosting of his ego rather than from helping the client to accomplish the changes required to enhance social functioning. If the worker's purpose is selfish, that is, if the worker's primary goal is to demonstrate personal competence and effectiveness, then the goals developed for the group may be inappropriate, even disastrous.

A thorough understanding of the above concepts and ideas does not necessarily provide all of the background knowledge for effective functioning in the group treatment process. Workers need to have a good understanding of themselves and of the influence they have on others, particularly on clients. Workers need to understand the ways in which they deal with issues of beginning, of authority, anger, hostility, appropriate affect, positive or negative regard, feelings of competence or incompetence and the very many issues of transference and counter-transference that will influence the group and the worker. It is possible that if workers are not aware of these aspects of themselves that they may, in times of stress, choose to change the topic under discussion not for the benefit of the client but for their own emotional well-being.

A sound knowledge base will help workers to identify and develop appropriate goals for specific groups and the goals will in turn influence how clients will be selected. Without a clear sense of purpose there is minimal focus or direction and this must influence the functioning of the group and may prevent it from benefitting from treatment. It is almost certain that a lack of purpose will lead to a lack of success.

QUESTIONS FOR CONSIDERATION

1. What factors should be considered in developing purposes for treatment groups?

2. What are the similarities and differences in the client population?

3. What basic knowledge does a worker need in order to lead a treatment group?

4. What impact would the client group have on developing the worker's purpose?

5. What personal motivation do you have for leading a treatment group?

6. What ways might your own needs, experience and aspirations affect your leadership style?

7. What are the characteristics of your potential group members?

8. Clearly identify the reasons why the treatment group is being set up from the following perspectives: (a) the organization (b) the client (c) the worker.

9. How might setting SMART goals direct the activities of the worker and client?

3

Factors That Determine the Selection of Group Members

The organizational context affects the development of the worker's purpose. In fact, the selection of the members of the treatment group is determined by the worker's purpose and the organizational context. However, there are many other factors that also affect the selection of members for treatment groups, factors such as: the worker's abilities, experience, knowledge; the specific client group; the problem and its context; and the planned treatment.

After the treatment purpose has been articulated for the group, decisions must be made about the program—decisions about emphases, approaches and techniques that are most likely to achieve the stated purposes. These decisions influence the kind of treatment program to be implemented.

Kind of Treatment Program

There are two broad types of group treatment programs, discussion and activity, but there can be, and generally is, a combination of programs in which the emphasis is on one or the other. A program's main thrust may be the cognitive or the affective functioning of the clients, but is certainly never one or the other! In fact, a *sine qua non* of group treatment is the development of the clients' problem-solving skills—a cognitive activity that can be and often is dependent on affective functioning. The worker may decide that an activity such as modeling in clay may be the best way to improve the affective functioning of a group of depressed clients, but this activity does not preclude discussion, such as the sharing of feelings and responses, or the evaluation of growth toward the achievement of objectives—especially if, as often happens, the depression (affective functioning) is retarding learning (cognition). In fact, discussion is an important part of the pre-affiliation stage; it is also the spring board of group decision making if problem solving is, as it should be, the worker's main objective.

Listening to guest speakers, reviewing films or asking questions, though not requiring the same level of physical involvement as clay modeling or badminton, is still an activity, although the emphasis may be on cognition rather than psycho-motor skills or abilities. After deciding on the pro-gram—that is, the activities and the emphases that are considered conducive to achieving the group's purposes and making decisions about whether the goals are mainly to improve cognition, affective functioning, behavioral skills or social functioning—the worker then determines the ex-tent of group input and the need for teaching aids such as films, recordings, lectures by guests, visits and tours. These decisions will in large measure determine:

- the type and size of the group;
- the frequency, number and length of meetings;
- the composition of the group; and
- the number of workers to be involved.

Organizations are established to meet specific societal and community needs and to serve specific client groups. The worker must function within these constraints and is expected to develop treatment goals that are in keeping with those of the organization. The organization is generally ori-ented toward specific treatment approaches. For example, the purpose of the medical hospital is to offer services to the physically ill and even though it may have a department or clinic where psychiatric problems are ad-dressed, it is not designed primarily to meet such needs. The principal role of the social work department in a medical facility is to help patients change and adapt to various aspects of their particular illness. Even though the medical facility may attempt to cope with some psychiatric problems, patients with severe mental disorders would normally be transferred to a psychiatric facility.

In the medical hospital the worker's purpose must be in keeping with that of the organization. In setting up the treatment group some possible goals could be to help a group of coronary patients accept their disability and devise ways of coping, or to prepare patients for major surgery. This will involve setting up groups that include patients with or without their families. There may be patients who have undergone surgery but are un-able to cope with the trauma of reduced functioning. The worker's purpose with this group could be:

- to improve their self-concept;
- to help them to recognize that although function is diminished, it is not lost;
- to motivate the group to maximize their functioning; and
- to alleviate the depression resulting from the traumatic experience.

Clearly, the worker's purpose is largely determined by the organizational context. The characteristics of the client group are also to some extent determined by the organizational context. For example, persons requesting service from a family service agency are likely to be seeking relief from difficulties that relate to family functioning. So the clients and their difficulties must be addressed within the constraints of the organization and the worker must then draw on personal resources (ability, knowledge, skills and experience) in order to decide on treatment purposes and the treatment most likely to achieve the planned purposes.

Type and Size of Group

Dorothy Whitaker (1975) notes that the group situation is likely to foster or encourage:

> social comparison, testing out new interactive behavior, learning interpersonal skills, learning to cooperate toward a shared goal, reassessing personal goals and values through comparing one's self with others, learning through modeling, learning through feedback, expanding one's own repertoire of behavior through observing others, alleviating isolation and loneliness. (p. 434)

For treatment purposes there are two types of groups, the *open group* and the *closed group*. In some situations the type of group is largely determined by the organization rather than the worker. Whereas the open group is more limited to personal responsibility for the achievement of individual goals, the closed group fosters and develops group decision-making and the achievement of personal goals through group interaction. In the closed group, personal growth is dependent on and enhanced by the group's development. The type of treatment offered is often determined by the organizational context, but the worker must make decisions about the most effective way of using the treatment process whether the group is closed or open.

Open Groups

The decision that clients enter or leave the group may be made by the worker, the organization or the client. This decision can be based on a number of factors such as the worker's evaluation of the client's progress, discharge from the particular treatment setting, the client's evaluation of personal needs, and the organization's policies and practices regarding intake. It is difficult to predetermine the duration of the individual's stay in the open group dependent as it is on the achievement of personal goals.

Closed Groups

In the closed group, membership is constant. The group generally meets for a specified length of time over a set period of time. No new members are admitted and group members are expected to attend each session for the duration of the treatment, which is usually pre-determined by a consensus of worker, client and organization.

The purpose of the closed group is the achievement of personal growth through group process. It is important that the composition of the group be maintained so that the group can develop as a system, with all its inherent strengths and weaknesses. If individual clients were allowed to enter and leave at will, the group's development would be retarded and in turn would adversely affect the achievement of group and individual goals.

In setting up a group, the worker must take into consideration the problems to be addressed, the needs of the client group, the constraints and resources of the organization and the purpose for which the treatment group is to be set up. For example, a group of clients whose common problem is the inability to establish and maintain close personal relationships, would find the treatment counter-productive in an open group where clients are allowed to move in and out of the group at will. Such a group would be unlikely to encourage or set the stage for members to experience the development of warm, trusting relationships. If such a group is to provide the maximum opportunity for learning and change, it would be necessary to have the same members interact with each other over a period of time.

Group Size

There is no consensus in the literature on the optimum size for an effective treatment group. There are several issues associated with varying group size. Group size determines the level of tension experienced, how and to what extent members interact and whether they will express disagreements. It is generally accepted that the smaller the group the higher the level of intimacy and interaction. Group size, in large measure, should be determined by the worker's purpose, but consideration must also be given to the specific problems and characteristics of the clients, the treatment approach to be used, the organizational context, and the skills and competence of the worker.

In treatment groups the most efficient size seems to be not less than five members and not more than nine. These numbers encourage optimum group interaction and intensity. The usual length of each session is one and a half to two hours. In some groups the treatment purpose may be facilitated by the provision of refreshments at the beginning or the end of the group session.

The worker in the medical hospital, whose purpose is to prepare patients for major heart surgery, may find that the size of the group is pre-determined. It is possible that there may only be two or three patients. In this context the size of the group is determined by the organization, although it may be more appropriate to have a larger group in order to minimize group tension and lower the level of patient anxiety. This example indicates how the size of the group may be determined by the situation. The success of group treatment would be dependent on the worker's ability and competence to assess the client group, the problem at hand and to devise the most effective and appropriate treatment. The worker who, from past experience, has found that seven to nine clients form an excellent group for diffusing tension and sharing experiences and fears may decide that it is important to have a larger group than the one suggested by the organization.

Decisions must then be made about enlarging the group and thereby altering its composition. Such decisions must be based on sound theories and relevant experiences. Taking into account the purpose for which the group is set up, the worker may decide on any or all of the following options:

- include close relatives;
- include former patients;
- include other patients preparing for major surgery; and
- include other patients recovering from major surgery.

Time as a Variable

Timing of worker interventions, the number of sessions to accomplish the tasks of the group and its members, and the duration of each phase of development, are difficult and complex aspects of group treatment. Generally, every time a group meets it goes through all of the phases of development in some limited form. Most of the issues around timing depend on the workers' skill and knowledge and his or her ability to make sound professional judgements about what stage the group and its members are at, at any given time.

If the number of sessions has been established by the sponsoring organization, the worker must then take into account the needs of the client group in general and specific terms, the coping abilities of the individual members, and decide how best to maximize the group process to meet the expressed needs. In such a scenario, the worker must help the group to establish a working contract as readily as is appropriate for the treatment tasks to begin. The earlier the worker can give the group responsibility for the work to be accomplished, the more quickly the group can move through its treatment phases. The worker, through the skillful use of the group contract, the ability to identify the themes presented in the group, and the ability to clarify, challenge, be supportive and project a professional self, can move the group through the phases of group development.

The worker must bear in mind that regardless of his skills and knowledge, groups often regress to earlier stages of development than the one in which they are working primarily. Such regression is a normal phenomenon of all human interactions. It is possible that some members may subconsciously influence the group process to move forward without perceiving that all members are not ready to go through the various treatment phases. The worker, using the affective process, may slow this movement. Timing of interventions, contracting, the limitations and abilities of all group members, the length of each session and the total number of sessions, are all critical in the group treatment process.

Kenneth Reid (1977) makes an excellent summary statement on timing:

> It is a naive misconception to view the effective role of the worker as unchanging; as the group develops and matures, different forms of leadership are required. Generally as a group evolves from a pre-group phase, through the formative, intermediate, maturation, and finally the termination phase, leadership changes from aiding the group with internal and external pressures, to helping the group itself to cope directly with these pressures. In the early phases the initial attraction to the group is fostered by the worker through his assistance to the members individually and collectively, in their search for common values and interests. His relationship to each of the members also serves to unify and to increase the group's attraction potential. In later phases this form of direct influence decreases with greater self-direction by the group due to the development of group norms, social control mechanisms, and operating and governing procedures. In the early phases the new member may need support and structure to stay in the group. If the worker confronts him with his "immature" behavior, he may force him out of the group. (pp. 11–12.)

Composition of the Group

In group selection consideration is often given to such client characteristics as commonality of problem and of purpose, homogeneity and heterogeneity.

Commonality of problem can be described as:

> Persons for whom a common need or problem has been identified should obviously be placed in the same group ... When all the group members have similar strivings, then their involvement in help to other members will have more direct meaning to their own problem

> solutions. There is a greater chance that the process will result in a
> group process toward problem-solution than that the group will sug-
> gest how one person can go about it. (Levine, 1965, p. 425.)

Those facing major surgery are likely to have a common need or problem. If the clients are grouped according to this common identifiable need
or problem the common purpose, from the worker's perception, could be
to relieve anxiety and help individual members cope with the situation.
Members facing a common problem identify with each other more quickly
and more easily. They tend to open themselves to each other and appear to
communicate their real selves more readily. Because the group uses its energies to solve the common problems, effort is maximized and the group as
a whole resolves the problems more efficiently.

Homogeneity/Heterogeneity

It is difficult to operationalize this concept because of the many variables
that can exist in any group. A few of these are race, culture, gender, experience, intelligence, social functioning and level of emotional maturity. For
this reason most groups are heterogeneous. A very real danger in selecting
members for the group is the possibility of having an isolate, a person who
because of a particular characteristic is vastly different from the rest of the
group. This characteristic may be related to intelligence, race, age, gender,
etc., but the person is isolated by the group and both the individual's and
the group's functioning can be impaired.

The worker's purpose derives from the organization's purpose. The client group is likely to have common needs and common problems.
Commonality of problem seems to be the most important criterion for
selection.

The Number of Workers to be Involved

In Chapter 10, consideration is given to leadership as a critical element
of th group's process. In some settings the organization expects several persons to be involved in the treatment process. For example, a nurse and a
social worker may be co-workers in a treatment group whose major purpose is to learn to accept and deal with loss of a limb or a specific body
function. The nurse would be expected to provide information, leadership
and guidance on medical and related matters while the social worker per-
forms a similar function in relation to psycho-social functioning. In order to
function effectively as co-workers these leaders must understand and to
some degree accommodate each other's philosophy and treatment approaches. At the same time, the co-workers individually and collectively
must go through the same preparatory processes outlined earlier. It would

be a mistake for one worker to do all the preparation for beginning the group with the other expecting to be effective without preparatory work. This could set the stage for misunderstanding and conflict to emerge during the group sessions, thus having a negative effect on the group's functioning. Both workers should be involved in all aspects of preparation including the pre-screening of potential group members.

Summary

The selection of members for group treatment is of utmost importance in determining the achievement of the goals of the individual client, of the workers and of the group as a whole. If adequate attention is not paid to the selection of members who are likely to benefit from the group experience, rather than helping to enhance the social competence of members, the group process may be disrupted. Workers must bear in mind that groups do not necessarily offer a panacea to all those who seek or are encouraged to enrol in them. Pre-screening provides an opportunity to assess a clients readiness to begin the group treatment process.

QUESTIONS FOR CONSIDERATION

1. Identify a specific client problem that would benefit from group treatment.

2. Plan a group treatment program that is likely to result in the resolution of the problem.

3. Indicate the type and size of the group; frequency, length and number of meetings.

4. What are the important factors to be considered when making decisions about the composition of a treatment group? How do these factors affect group development and functioning?

5. In preparing for a treatment group led by two workers, how should the preparatory tasks be assigned?

6. What criteria should determine a worker's decision to change the size and composition of a group predetermined by the organization?

7. What criteria should be used for deciding on the type of treatment group?

4

Pre-Screening—Its Relevance to Treatment

There is no agreed upon position expressed in current social group work literature on the matter of pre-screening clients for inclusion in groups designed to provide treatment. It is the author's belief, based on experience in conducting groups, that pre-screening has the potential to maximize the opportunities for clients to change during the life of a treatment group. Pre-screening may be seen as the final preparatory step before the first group session.

The pre-screening of clients is sometimes referred to as pre-group contact (Glassman and Kates, 1990). This activity may be conducted either formally or informally depending on the organization under whose auspices group treatment is practiced and the purpose for which the group is planned. It provides an opportunity for the worker to use his or her experience and theoretical knowledge to select members for the client group based on an assessment of their ability to work together toward the resolution of the problem. Furthermore, it provides opportunity for the worker to assess his level of comfort and competence in dealing with a particular client and problem.

In a recent text on group work by Glassman and Kates (1990) the point is made that the worker, as representative of the agency, should be prepared to respond in a direct manner to all questions related to the purpose and he functioning of the group. In addition, the concerns that potential members bring to the group and the anxieties attendant on this new experience should be addressed in a forthright manner. In order to arrest many of the clients' fears and anxieties, the worker should help them to understand what group participation means and the process and rules by which the group will proceed.

Risks

Glassman and Kates aptly outline the purpose of pre-screening and suggest how it might be done. The worker and the group are exposed to certain risks if pre-screening is not built into the group treatment process. Some of these risks are:

1. *No opportunity for the worker to assess the readiness of the client for the treatment experience.*

   Without pre-screening the worker is unlikely to have adequate information on which to assess the client's readiness for the treatment experience. The more difficult the problem confronting the client the greater the probability that the client will feel overwhelmed and unable to focus on the steps necessary to effect positive change. During pre-screening the worker has the opportunity to elicit information about previous experiences and help the client to recognize that a problem can be solved if it is approached in well defined manageable segments. For example, a client may indicate that he or she feels overwhelmed by circumstances in their life. Such an identification of the problem is too generalized and unmanageable as a focus for work in the group. During pre-screening, the worker can assist the client in identifying the feelings, thoughts, behavior and possible causes for feeling overwhelmed and then to determine which segment should be the immediate focus of treatment. With assistance from the worker the client is helped to explore the situation and make a commitment to enter the treatment process. Moreover, the certainty of having a specific manageable goal to achieve is likely to facilitate clients' movement through the change process. More work is therefore possible in the time allotted for treatment.

2. *No information of the client's ability to handle effectively the pressures of a group.*

   Pre-screening provides the opportunity for the worker to assess the client's eligibility for group treatment and to determine whether the client has the capacity to withstand group pressures or not. It is essential to the well-being of the client and of the group that each member of the group has the capacity to set personal limits and boundaries and not be swayed by the group as a collectivity by the leader or by individual members. Such susceptible individuals are unlikely to be able to function as effective group members.

   In order to facilitate personal change, each member, at various times throughout the life of the group, must be able to stand apart from the group while at the same time using the support provided by the group for implementing the desired change. For example, a client may enter the group with a tendency to be introverted. If the group were to develop, as one of its norms, the idea that each individual be expected to share personal information, an introverted client would find it difficult and even impossible to follow this rule. In such a scenario, the client may opt out of the treatment process and could in fact short-circuit the treatment process.

3. *No information regarding the client's ability to verbalize his or her needs, problems or concerns. Hence the question: will the client be able to function in the group situation?*

   If clients are admitted into groups without pre-screening it is possible that some of them may not have the ability to verbalize their needs, problems or concerns in the group. The group is not a panacea for all personal ills. To receive help in a group an individual must be able to participate effectively in the life and work of the group. This requires interaction with others by way of listening, giving feedback and expressing one's thoughts and feelings about what is going on at any given time. An inability to participate in this way indicates that the individual client will find it difficult to function in the group situation for either personal benefit or the development of the group.

4. *No knowledge of the client's voluntary or involuntary status on entering the group.*

   Without pre-screening it would be difficult to determine whether the clients involvement in the group is voluntary or involuntary. This does not refer specifically to the legal status of the client on entering the group, but to what extent is it the decision of the client to seek treatment of his or her own volition. If the client feels that he or she has been coerced, then the workers intervention ought to be directed toward preparing the client for treatment rather than entering the treatment process immediately.

5. *No understanding as to whether the group experience is likely to be helpful to the client or not.*

   Without pre-screening there is minimal opportunity for either client or worker to examine whether the group treatment modality is likely to be beneficial to the client. There needs to be some exploration of how the presenting problem of the client may lend itself to identification, analysis and possible change in the group context. Psycho-social problems that are evident when the client interacts with others are likely to surface during pre-screening.

   From discussion during pre-screening it may become evident that the problems of some clients cannot be addressed in a group treatment modality. The purposes for which group treatment is designed are to effect some specific changes in the clients affective, cognitive and or behavioral states. To maximize the benefits of group treatment for each client, the process of identifying the problem and the specific change goals to be achieved should begin prior to the first group session, since few if any treatment groups are designed to meet indefinitely.

Benefits

On the other hand, there appear to be several benefits for the client, the worker and to the group treatment process if pre-screening is done. Workers should consider the benefits that accrue from pre-screening. These benefits are:

1. *The worker gains a beginning understanding of the client in relation to the problem and the psycho-social context.*

   Pre-screening provides the worker with the opportunity to understand how the client perceives the specific problem and, at the same time, how the client is coping. The information should be used by the worker to anticipate themes that are likely to arise during the various stages of group development and how best he or she can help the individuals as part of the group system to work effectively with the themes in order to facilitate individual change. Moreover, this information can provide knowledge to both client and practitioner of the possible difficulties likely to be encountered as group treatment is pursued.

   Potential clients are often referred because of a common problem. Alcohol abuse, for example, can be addressed through group treatment. Alcohol abuse may be the only common problem among potential group members, who may vary in age, sex, experience, ethnicity, economic status, and in social, psychological and developmental competence. If there is great disparity, for example, in age or economic status among group members, treatment can be severely limited. The curative factors inherent in group treatment—that is, the development of intimacy, cohesion, trust, universality, and the installation of hope—will be almost impossible to achieve.

2. *The process of worker/client joining that is vital to the development of such therapeutic factors as cohesion, trust, intimacy, the installation of hope, are initiated. This will facilitate client change through group development.*

   Pre-screening gives the worker and client the opportunity to explore with each other how they can be mutually helpful in working toward the achievement of the client's goals and the ongoing development of the group. As the client enters the group he or she feels less alone and isolated since there has already been some purposeful interaction. With pre-screening the client is able to begin to trust the worker and to feel that the problem is understandable and manageable. The development of trust enables the client to risk interacting with others, thereby creating an environment that facilitates personal change.

The interaction that occurs during pre-screening will facilitate a more effective start of the treatment group. Because of this interaction dialoguing during the first group session is enhanced along with the search to identify and articulate individual and group goals as members begin to understand the purposes for which the group is convened.

3. *The element of surprise is minimized as the group begins its work. The client is able to deal more effectively with the normal anxieties of a new situation—the beginning of the group—and is better able to confront the concerns and issues attendant on entry to the group.*

Knowing what to expect throughout the treatment process helps the client to decide if he or she is willing to make a public commitment to work toward the achievement of individual treatment goals. Pre-screening gives the client an overview of how the group treatment process will unfold and the role each client is expected to play in order for change to occur. Without this knowledge clients are surprised by the unfolding of the dynamic group process, and may feel unsure of themselves and choose to withdraw from treatment.

After the worker has outlined what is likely to occur during the life of the group and how the client may experience the process, the client sees the practitioner as having credibility and therefore as trustworthy. When clients perceive that the practitioner is competent, they will be more willing to give of themselves when dealing with the normal anxieties of beginning a new experience. Pre-screening can be seen as analogous to being given a map of the journey to personal and group change.

4. *The opportunity for worker and client to identify some of their personal and professional limitations and necessary boundaries.*

Worker and client alike approach the group with varying degrees of anxiety and ambivalence about the new situation. Each has real and imaginary expectations of the other. The worker hopes that the client knows what the problem is, is motivated to work with others on the problem, that the client will be able to set appropriate goals and have the capacity to work effectively toward achieving the desired goals. The client, on the other hand, expects that by beginning the treatment process the worker will, through some magical means, achieve on his or her behalf the desired goals.

Pre-screening gives both worker and client the opportunity to explore the various roles that each is expected to play as part of the treatment process. The worker can explore earlier life experiences of the client in order to determine the capacities and resources available to the client to work in a group toward the achievement of the desired goals. At the same time the worker should clearly and thoughtfully outline his or her facilitative role.

Such a role should be to provide acceptance, understanding and caring as the clients confront and deal with problems and concerns. The practitioner's role as a magician must be demystified, so that the client can be helped to assume major responsibility for the program, the treatment goals to be established and the work necessary to achieve the goals. In this way the worker plays a major role in identifying, clarifying, setting and establishing the boundaries that both client and worker should follow as the group process unfolds.

5. *To enable the worker to evaluate/assess clients understanding, knowledge and experiences considered relevant to treatment processes.*

Files from other workers and referrals seldom give adequate information about clients' strengths, limitations, understandings, knowledge and experiences. The less the worker knows about the client and his or her history the more difficult it will be to determine effective group interventions.

Pre-screening provides an opportunity for the worker to test some beginning hypotheses regarding the client's understanding of the group process. Much of the client's understanding and knowledge of groups is based on myth and rumor. Intervention at pre-screening if competently done allows the worker to help the client to get a realistic picture of how the group will unfold and the contribution that each member can make in order to achieve the established treatment goals. Since most members are unlikely to have had a group treatment experience, by elaborating on the process that is likely to unfold the worker allays some of the client's legitimate fears and anxieties at the beginning of a new experience. A client who does not understand group process at some basic level may not be able to gain the necessary insights, while in the group, to effectively work on his or her problem or issue.

In addition the worker can help clients who have not entered group treatment before to see the relevance of their family life to the present treatment situation. This activity pays off for the worker in that through it he or she gains credibility that can enhance the development of the curative factors in the group.

6. *The opportunity for exploring and defining goals before the treatment process begins.*

Most human beings have difficulty defining and articulating their life goals. This task is even more difficult for persons overwhelmed by life crises and in need of professional help. During pre-screening the worker can help the client to review the areas of difficulty and to begin to set realistic, manageable and achievable treatment goals. In order to set treatment goals with the client the various aspects of the problem must be identified and appropriate and specific goals must be established for each aspect of the problem. This process, conducted during pre-screening, should include some beginning prioritizing of the goals and some feedback on how the goals may be achieved in the group.

This initial goal setting process helps the client to see that life crises are manageable and need not be overwhelming. Further, the process attempts to instill a sense of hope in the client that allows for some commitment to treatment. Any effort that helps in the development of the therapeutic or curative factors is of significant benefit to client change and group development. The orderly pursuit of individual and group treatment goals is an essential ingredient in the achievement of such goals.

Pre-screening provides an opportunity for the worker to use his or her experience and theoretical knowledge to select members for the client group based on an assessment of their ability to work together toward the resolution of the problem. It also provides opportunity for the worker to assess his or her level of comfort and competence in dealing with a particular client and problem.

Summary

The purposes of pre-screening or pre-group contact are to evaluate, inform, allay fears and anxieties, begin to establish a climate of trust and acquire an understanding of the client. Hence, a pre-screening interview should be designed to achieve the following objectives:

- to assess the client's problems, goals and needs in relation to the purpose of the group;
- to assess the client's ability to take responsibility for the problem;
- to acquaint the client with the worker's role and functioning during the treatment process;
- to evaluate the kinds of group experiences and family relationships that the client has had;
- to inform the client of the planned group experience and the expectations of clients in the group;
- to evaluate the client's suitability for the group experience;
- to establish a climate of trust with individual members of the group;

- to allow the worker to evaluate and come to terms with his or her own responses to the client's problems and the client group;

- to address the client's and the worker's anxieties about the planned group experience; and

- to provide an opportunity for the client to ask questions about the planned treatment.

The pre-screening process does not necessarily indicate who should be in the group but should give some indications as to those persons who should be excluded. Persons to be excluded should be those whose inclusion would be likely to create a significant imbalance in the function of the group. Significant imbalance may be caused by persons likely to be made scapegoats because they are significantly different from other group members. If attention is not paid to the factors that may create imbalance in a group, tensions may develop that could render the group dysfunctional. Finally, one should keep in mind that, given the dynamics of the client's problem or problems, it is possible that he or she may not be able to give accurate personal information during pre-screening.

QUESTIONS FOR CONSIDERATION

1. What are the benefits to be achieved by pre-screening clients for group treatment?

2. What factors would indicate that inclusion in a group may not be in the client's best interest?

3. How should pre-screening be conducted for group treatment?

4. What ought to be the primary underlying philosophy for pre-screening clients?

SECTION 1: SUGGESTED READINGS

- Barnes, G.G. (1975). Deprived adolescents: A use for group work. *British Journal of Social Work, 5,* 149–160.

- Bennis, W.G., Benne, K.D., Chin, R., and Corey, K.E. (Eds.). (1976). *The Planning of Change (3rd ed.).* New York: Holt, Rinehart and Winston.

- Bernstein, S. (Ed.). (1965). *Explorations in Social Group work.* Boston: Boston University, School of Social Work.

- Bradford, L.G., (Ed.). (1978). *Group Development (2nd ed.).* La Jolla, California: University Associates.

- Compton, B., and Galaway, B. (1984). *Social Work Processes (3rd ed.).* Illinois: The Dorsey Press.

- Corey, G., and Corey, M.S. (1982). *Groups: Process and Practice (2nd ed.).* Monterey, California: Brooks and Cole Publishing Co.

- Empey, L.J. (1977). Clinical group work with multi-handicapped adolescents. *Social Casework.* 58, 593–599.

- Garland, J., and West, J. (1964). Differential assessment and treatment of the school age child: Three group approaches. *Social Work with Groups, 7(4),* 57–70.

- Garvin, C.D. (1981). *Contemporary Group Work.* New Jersey: Prentice-Hall Inc.

- Garvin, C.D. (1984). The changing contexts of social group work practice: Challenge and opportunity. *Social Work with Groups, 7(1),* 3–19.

- Golden, N., Chirlin, P., and Shone, B. (1979). Tuesday children. *Social Casework, 51,* 599–605.

- Goodman, K., and Rothman, B. (1984). Group work in infertility treatment. *Social Work with Groups, 7(1),* 79–97.

- Hartford, M.E., and Parsons, R. (1982). Uses of groups with relatives of dependent older adults. *Social Work with Groups, 5(2),* 77–90.

- Heap, K. (1984). Purposes in social work with groups: Their interrelatedness with values and methods—A historical and prospective view. *Social Work with Groups, 7(1),* 21–54.

- Kell, B.L., and Mueller, W.J. (1966). *Impact and Change: A Study of Counseling Relationships.* New Jersey: Prentice-Hall Inc.

- Klein, A.F. (1972). *Effective Group Work.* New York: Association Press.

- Levine, B. (1965). Principles for developing an ego supportive group treatment service. *Journal of Social Service Review, 39.*

- Monane, J.H. (1967). *A Sociology of Human Systems.* New York: Appleton Century Crofts.

- Reid, K.E. (1977). Worker authenticity in group work. *Clinical Journal of Social Work, 5,* 3–16.

- Ross, A.L., and Bernstein, N.D. (1976). A framework for the therapeutic use of group activities. *Child Welfare,* 55(9), 627–640.

- Schwartz, W., and Zalba, S. (1975). *The Practice of Group Work.* New York: Columbia University Press.

- Shulman, L. (1968). *A Casebook of Social Work with Groups: The Mediating Model.* New York: Council on Social Work Education.

- Shulman, L. (1979). *The Skills of Helping Individuals and Groups.* Itasca, Illinois: Peacock Publishers Inc.

- Trecker, H.B. (1972). *Social Group Work: Principles and Practices.* New York: Association Press.

- Whitaker, D.W. (1975). Some conditions for effective work with groups. *British Journal of Social Work, 5(4),* 421–439.

STAGES OF GROUP DEVELOPMENT

his section is organized according to the stages of development presented by Garland, Jones and Kolodny (1965). Using the five stages
some of the interventions that would enhance workers practice are
indicated. There is no suggestion that this is a blueprint for practice, but
rather it should be considered as a means of consciously and deliberately
using theory to inform practice.

Be aware that the practitioner's intervention that is appropriate during
one stage may have disastrous results at another stage. It is usual in practice
with groups to have two workers in co-leadership roles. Co-leadership
presents its own issues and challenges for practitioners since the two workers are likely to exhibit the same characteristics of development as those
within of the larger group.

SECTION 2: CONTENTS

5

Worker Concerns and Intervention During Pre-Affiliation

A number of individuals, pre-screened for treatment by the worker, now need to get to know each other and the worker to share their common goals and purposes. As they do, they establish the social-emotional climate that will allow them to achieve their goals as a group. This first stage is referred to as *pre-affiliation* and it may spread over three or more sessions.

Pre-affiliation is the beginning stage of group development, characterized by:

- Rituals;
- Anxiety, uncertainty, doubts and fears;
- No close ties, hence dialoguing;
- Non-intimate relationships;
- Use of past experiences;
- Approach-avoidance;
- Confidentiality;
- Explorations and affiliations; and
- Contracting (Garland, Jones and Kolodny, 1965).

The worker's first task is to help all members of this beginning treatment group to articulate clearly their purposes for being in the group and the commitments they are prepared to make toward the successful achievement of their individual and collective group goals. These goals and purposes should be complementary to the overall goals and purposes of the organization under whose auspices the treatment process is initiated and implemented.

The worker should recognize and be aware that it is normal for human beings to experience tensions and anxieties in new situations. In order to minimize some of the stresses of beginning the group, the worker using the problem-solving sequence may begin to provide the group with some structure that will facilitate its work. One way of providing this structure would be for the worker to welcome all members to the group, briefly out-line his or her understanding of the group's purpose and follow this by a contextual introduction. The worker should in fact model for the group members how best to introduce themselves to each other. The introduction ought to indicate the worker's general purpose for the group, the kinds of group experiences planned, the specific tasks and the expectations for members of the group and for the group as a whole.

Depending on the purpose and skill of the worker, several options are possible to enable group members to tell something of themselves and learn something of each other. Several beginning games have been devel-oped, often referred to as icebreakers. A very effective way of beginning the treatment process is for the worker, following his or her own introduc-tion, to ask each member of the group to give his or her name; to briefly tell the group the concerns that bring them to this particular group; what they personally hope to achieve by attending this group; what expectations they have of each other, including the worker; and what type of contribution and commitment the group can expect from them.

A response by a group member to such a request for information could be: *My name is Ann. Six months ago my husband deserted me and our three chil-dren. Our marriage was not the greatest, but we were getting along in a fashion. He left us for another woman. Since then, I feel very disorganized. The children are holy terrors and I don't seem to be managing very well financially.* Ann is restless in her chair and fidgets with her handbag. After a deep breath she continues with her introduction: *I want to be a good parent and stand on my own feet financially. Right now this seems impossible. I would like to learn about myself from the experi-ences of others and will share my life experiences with all of you if I feel comfortable enough. I will make every effort to attend each session and actively participate, if I'm not criticized too much.*

The worker now has several options for intervention. These options are: to normalize Ann's situation in light of the concerns or problems of other members; to indicate how and the extent to which her expectations are likely to be met; to ask the group if any of its members share similar con-cerns, issues or problems; to identify the major themes underlying Ann's introduction, making an effort to hook other members into these themes; and to suggest how these themes may be dealt with in the group.

Identifying the themes introduced by each member during or after the introductions indicates that the worker has been listening to what the cli-ents have been saying. At this time in the life of the group the identified themes are rather general and often couched in vague terms. From these general themes, the worker can guide the group members toward more specific themes. The specific themes should embody aspects of cognition, affect and behavior that the clients seek to change.

The themes that may be identified from Ann's introduction are: feelings of rejection and abandonment; inadequacy as a spouse and parent; poor self image; anxiety; fears about the future and aspects of depression and loss. On the other hand, Ann also presents such themes as sensitivity to others, willingness to learn from others and to share her experiences with others. It is the responsibility of the worker to recognize the various themes that are presented and to connect verbally and non-verbally those members with similar themes. The objective here is to begin the process of bonding members to each other and ultimately to the group. It is likely that the members of the group have not met prior to their first group session. They must, therefore, be helped to relate to each other in a manner that would produce cohesion and create an environment of trust so that they may be willing to share their abilities and limitations. It is through the sharing of concerns, issues and problems, through a recognition of the commonality of these, and of the themes raised in the group, that the treatment process is begun.

Group treatment will be facilitated if the worker is able to help the group members clearly articulate and order the themes that are to be critically examined. The worker's role is that of helping the group to structure its activity and discussion in a problem-solving sequence. Knowledge of the group as a beginning social system and the elements of the pre-affiliation stage of group development will help the worker to perform in an effective manner. Worker effectiveness will depend on the ability to help the group identify common themes, develop a climate of safety and trust so that members are not penalized for taking risks and, at the same time, promote interaction and honest sharing among all members of the group.

The identification of themes is critical in any treatment process. Hearing the themes allows the worker to intervene in a manner that highlights the affective aspects of the client's past and current functioning. Such a process addresses not only the words that are spoken, but also the metaphorical significance of both verbal and non-verbal communication.

For example, it is significant that Ann paused after saying: "I will share my life experiences with all of you." The significance of this pause indicates hesitancy, a feeling that Ann may not be able to live up to the commitment she had made. This is reinforced in the qualifying statement: "If I feel comfortable enough!" This may indicate anxiety or a lack of self confidence. These themes have been identified on the basis of both verbal and non-verbal communication. There may be other themes apparent through gestures and body language.

While content and process are important in their own right, content acts as a mirror from and through which process can be understood. When information is shared in the group, meaning is derived from it, an interpretation of the relationship among group members is possible and themes may be identified. Attending to content gives the worker a sense of the process and how it may be affected for the growth and change of the member in a treatment group.

In the example cited from the information that Ann shares, meaning can be derived. Signs of discomfort, embarrassment, indifference or disgust are indications of the group's response to Ann's statement and how it was made. This will be an indication of how these members have historically dealt with the problem. On the basis of this information, the worker may identify themes on which treatment will be focused.

The content was what Ann said, namely the information she shared. The way in which she said it, revealed underlying themes–the affect. The way in which the information was given and received is the essence of the communication–the process. The worker will concentrate on the themes revealed by the process and its acceptance by the group in an effort to help the group members deal with their problem.

Through systematically modeling for such clients as Ann, the worker helps group members to see and understand that they too can identify their issues, concerns or problems and themes; focus on some aspect of them; examine their feelings, thoughts, behavior and experiences around the areas of concern; identify possible options for change, recognizing the attendant consequences and then choose an option. Clients should also be helped to evaluate the long-term effect of their choices. Success in group treatment is enhanced if, by the end of the pre-affiliation stage, there is among all members of the group a clear sense of what is to be accomplished and how it will be accomplished.

Rituals

Human beings have developed set ways of beginning relationships with each other. Each member brings his own rituals to the group and these can help or hinder the development of relationships. Rituals are cues that help the worker to assess the individual's life experiences and predict how that person is likely to function in the group. Embodied in the ritual of beginnings are ways of introducing one's self and establishing contact. The worker's eliciting rituals to a large extent set the tone for the group. The worker should so structure the beginning rituals that the commonality of issues and concerns is established in a manner that members recognize and accept this commonality. For example, the worker's eliciting rituals could include informing the members of the purpose of the organization, of the worker's purpose and expectations and his or her expectations of the group. As part of the introduction ritual the worker can ask members of the group to state their purpose and expectations for being there. In so doing the worker serves as a model by taking the initiative and demonstrating what is expected. Conversely, if the worker gives and solicits personal information unrelated to the purpose for being there, instead of establishing the commonality of purpose, the differences among individuals will be highlighted, differences in characteristics such as age, occupation, family background or education. This is likely to create doubt and tensions rather than reinforce the common purpose.

Anxiety, Uncertainty, Doubts and Fears

Anxiety is a normal response to new situations. Most human beings experience apprehension and fear when they are expected to discuss their problems and concerns with others, particularly strangers. The uncertainty about the group treatment experience, the anticipated or perceived reactions of the worker and others in the group are likely to heighten an individual's anxiety. It becomes imperative that the worker recognize that there will be anxiety and that through a certain level of anxiety treatment will be enhanced. To exceed this level, however determined, will hinder the individual and the group in the achievement of their goals and objectives.

It is important to recognize that some circumstances or actions, either planned or spontaneous, can raise the level of anxiety in the group to a point that will work against the group's functioning. For example, the physical setting in which the group meets; insensitive confrontation of a member by the worker or another group member; failure of the worker to identify the stage of group development; attempts to accelerate or retard the group's development; failure to acknowledge the contribution of individuals; and perceived incompetence of the worker or perceived favoritism by the worker to one or more members could raise the level of anxiety.

"No Close Ties" Dialoguing

When a treatment group is established, it is likely that none of the members will know each other. For some members, social interactions may be difficult because they have not developed or practiced beginning rituals that they can use to establish contact with strangers. Some persons find it easy to introduce themselves and begin conversation, for others this is very difficult.

The only group member that everyone may have had contact with is the worker, the group leader. It is the worker's responsibility to recognize that dialoguing will occur as individuals are likely to attempt to relate to the worker and not to each other. The worker's task here is to find and use common themes and common threads that link members together so that they are helped to establish and develop ties and relationships among themselves. If close ties can be developed then it is conceivable that, as the group moves through other phases of its development, these bonds will create the cohesion that will allow members to feel more comfortable in the group situation, and more comfortable about risking exposure of their weaknesses and limitations as they seek to learn about themselves and others, and move toward the accomplishment of the group's purposes.

Non-Intimate Relationships

We can expect that during the beginning phase of the group's life the clients will not be able to develop intimate relationships. The rituals that the clients use are a means of getting acquainted yet they want to maintain some distance and protect themselves. The rituals are frequently seen in what is referred to as small talk, discussion about inconsequential matters as they relate to one's lifestyle and one's ability to interact with others. Clients may also use the ritual of humor when the content under discussion gets to be too personal or threatening. These are ways of deflecting the group through the use of humorous comments or statements or through suggestions for new directions for discussion.

If the worker is unable to recognize the need for establishing non-intimate relationships at this stage he or she may unwittingly push group members to disclose more than they are able or ready to disclose at the time, and this may cause members to feel pressured and vulnerable and hence reluctant to return for another session. In spite of the need for non-intimate relationships the worker must demonstrate, through the use of simple problem-solving techniques, how the various issues that arise in the group will be dealt with. This must be done in a mildly confronting though supportive, warm and caring manner. Individuals should be encouraged and be given every opportunity to express themselves without fear of any criticism or ridicule.

Use of Past Experiences

In any group, members come with a variety of experience. Apart from the commonality of the problem there will be variations of the problems and concerns for each member. Some members may have had previous experience with the group treatment process, for others it may be a new experience. Differences will also exist in the level of social-emotional development, the perceptions and expectations of the group experience, of the worker and of the process.

The worker brings to the group his experiences, specifically experiences with previous groups. Some of these will be positive, others negative. Each worker must try to avoid the transfer of negative feelings and impressions to the new group. At the same time the worker must recognize and utilize, where appropriate, the collective experiences for the benefit of the group. For example, the worker may initiate a discussion around past group treatment experiences and encourage those without such experiences to seek information about the process. In this way, the worker attempts to create bonds among members, encouraging both participation and interaction.

Approach-Avoidance

All members of a treatment group bring with them certain apprehensions and misconceptions about being in a group. Clients are aware of their perceived inadequacies and are often concerned about revealing such inadequacies in what may be considered a public forum. At the same time there is a strong need to use the opportunity to get whatever assistance is available to remedy or deal with the problems they face. Such ambivalence is normal during the pre-affiliation stage. The client wants to be part of the group treatment process but at the same time feels the need to withdraw to protect the ego. Initially, clients may volunteer more information than they intend and then try to withdraw from the group in order to protect themselves. This behavior, though defensive, is very appropriate and necessary during the pre-affiliation stage. It is imperative that the worker understands the need for and normalcy of this phenomenon and takes steps to create an environment that would make it safe, even though not necessarily comfortable, for the individual to share concerns and not feel vulnerable during the process.

To do this, the worker may bring the member back into the group by asking what the feelings were as he shared the particular information. Following this, it would be necessary to elicit from the group their reactions and feelings about the information that was shared. This is difficult at most times but particularly at the beginning of the group treatment process. The worker's thrust then is to build in safety for self-disclosure and to begin to establish the type and extent of self-disclosure that is acceptable. For example, the worker may acknowledge the contribution of a member around some personal content, thank the member for being as open as he or she was and then seek the reactions of all members to the disclosure and invite others to share in a like manner or modify their disclosures appropriately.

The emphasis during this beginning phase is on learning through modeling, whether the model is that of the worker or a group member. In a group for pre-delinquent girls, one of the members shared that she had been sexually abused by her mother's boyfriend several days earlier. The group was quiet as "A" related her story.

Worker: *That must have been very upsetting for you. It must have been difficult for you to share that with us.*

A: *Yes. I wonder if I did the right thing!*

Worker: *Thank you for sharing it. I wonder how the rest of you feel about what A said to us! Could you share your feelings with us?* and later: *Is that the kind of information we want to share with each other? And is that how we can share it? A has provided a model for us that will be tough to follow. What do you think?*

At the same time, the worker must assess the needs of each client by making some judgments about the strengths or weaknesses of the individual clients and his or her ability to deal with the issues before the group in relation to his or her own change and development. Some decisions must also be made about the extent to which the abilities of the individual can be used to help others in the treatment process.

Confidentiality

In the group treatment process, clients are encouraged to share personal information as part of their treatment. It is, therefore, the responsibility of the organization, the worker and the group to ensure that this information remains confidential. This means that specific information about members should not be shared outside of the group or organization unless there are explicit directives (known to all) regarding the sharing of such information.

At the group level, the worker has to ensure that all members understand and are committed to the principle of confidentiality. This principle is based on the mutual respect of worker and members for each other. A safe environment for treatment is dependent on the extent to which the clients perceive the group, the worker and the organization as committed to confidentiality. Discussion and assurance of confidentiality should begin during pre-screening and be emphasized whenever the material under discussion warrants it; thus ensuring that there is understanding and commitment to this basic principle of group treatment. Confidentiality should not only apply to the worker and the members of the group, but anyone who observes, records or reviews group sessions should respect and adhere to this principle. In fact clients should be told how their information will be used. As material is presented by members, the worker should help the group to identify if that specific kind of information should be dealt with in a confidential manner. Confidentiality will develop if it is built on mutual respect for the privacy and feelings of each group member.

Exploration and Affiliation

An important part of pre-affiliation is to introduce and establish the problem-solving construct as the *modus operandi* of the group treatment process. The worker's purpose is to help the clients develop the ability to solve their problems rather than to present them with a worker-devised solution. To do this the worker must encourage client-client interactions as well as worker-client interactions. It is by examining the type and level of interaction within the group that the worker is able to help group members identify problems that may or may not have been verbalized.

Cohesive bonds are developed through the sharing and exploration of problems, issues, concerns and themes. This involves self-disclosure, sharing, and risking one's self with others. It provides the opportunity for the clients to learn from each other and be supportive of each other. This process of exploration and affiliation helps the participants to learn what is acceptable and what is not, and also to get feedback that is based on reality. This exploration ought to be so structured that the group is guided through the problem-solving sequence.

The following is an example of exploration and affiliation. A member of a group has stated that for him communication presents a problem. He has said that he finds it difficult to express ideas and feelings. If this is really a problem it will become evident as the client interacts with others in the group. In other words, the problem will surface in the group. The worker is then presented with an opportunity to explore this specific difficulty using the problem-solving approach and communication then becomes a group problem rather than the problem of a specific member. All the members have an opportunity to examine problems related to communication and to participate to the best of their ability in solving the communication problem for themselves and for others.

Difficulty with communication by a member of a group of separated parents may be exhibited in statements such as the following:

Sue: *I cannot get through to my kids since my husband left. They don't listen to me. I am at my wit's end.*

Such a statement should first be,

- acknowledged by the worker or another group member;
- the themes in the statement should be identified;
- clarification should be sought as to whether the themes are specific to the member or to the group; and
- a working group contract should be established.

Such a statement may be interpreted by the worker in several ways, depending on his or her theoretical orientation. Sue may be finding it difficult communicating clear messages to her children; she may not be recognizing the stages of development through which her children may be going; she may be grieving the loss of her spouse; she may not be recognizing her children's feelings of loss; she may be feeling inadequate as a parent; or any combination of the above. Several themes emerge from Sue's statement, offering several possible responses by the worker.

At this beginning stage in the group's development, the worker should acknowledge Sue's statement, for example: *Sue, it must have taken great courage for you to have told us that. I admire you for sharing it with us. How did the rest of you feel, as Sue shared this information?* After the other members respond, Sue could be asked to give examples (affective, cognitive and behavioral) to support her earlier statement. In this way, the worker could help Sue and the group identify the themes raised in her statement and determine to what extent these themes are specific to Sue alone or are applicable to others in the group. After acknowledging the statement, the worker could continue: *Sue, it sounds as though you have several concerns about how things are going for you. Do others of you share similar concerns? For example, are you unable to communicate well with others? Do you at times feel inadequate as a parent? Do you feel pain or hurt at the loss of your partners? Sue has demonstrated for us how we can talk about such concerns.* If the themes are general for others, the worker may seek agreement from them and have the group discuss how these themes may be discussed and in what order.

Another option would be for the group to decide that Sue's concerns are generally not theirs but note that they would like to give her feedback and comments about the way they have dealt with similar situations. In addition, the group may ask Sue if she would be prepared to do the same thing with other members when they shared concerns that were not of particular relevance or interest to her. In this scenario, one of the members could make the following comment: *I have difficulty being polite to my ex-spouse. I would like to know how I am seen by the rest of you. I need your feedback and comment.*

Worker: *Are we all agreeable to discuss the issues and concerns we have outlined so far, with each one sharing and participating? How do you feel about such a plan?*

In this way, the worker may skillfully help the group to develop a part of its working contract around some of the themes to be discussed in the group, without singling out Sue or doing one-to-one treatment in the group context.

Contracting

One of the primary objectives to be achieved during the pre-affiliation stage is the development of a working agreement or contract, understood and accepted by all members of the group. The term "contract" is best avoided when working with clients, as the legal connotations are likely to raise their level of anxiety unnecessarily and impede group process. There must be some agreement on:

- what the group is committing itself to do;
- how each member will assist in helping the group to achieve its treatment goals;
- the expectations of the organization;
- the expectations of the worker; and
- the expectations of each group member.

The contracting process must be explicit around such issues as: confidentiality; participation by group members; how other relationships between members will be used; the recording procedures used by the organization, by the worker and by the client; how the group will accomplish its purpose; the times and place of group sessions; and the length and number of sessions.

Summary

Pre-affiliation is a beginning stage in the life of the group. The worker needs to recognize the kinds of experiences and feelings that are associated with beginnings and help the clients to associate this experience with past and future beginnings. Just as beginnings create and are associated with emotions such as anxiety and fear, endings and closure present similar difficulties that must be addressed. The worker must be aware that even as the group is beginning, the process of termination has begun. As the group goes through its beginning phase, the various issues of each member must be clearly articulated as well as the member's purpose or goals for group treatment.

The major tasks to be accomplished by the worker during this pre-affiliation stage are:

- to establish a safe, but not necessarily comfortable, working environment for the treatment process;
- to clearly agree what is to be accomplished and how the work of the group is to be accomplished; and
- to demonstrate competence in his or her ability to lead the group through this phase of development.

As the worker leads the group through the pre-affiliation stage it must be recognized that the needs of each individual are as important as the needs of the group and of the organization. If the group is able to accomplish the tasks of this stage successfully, then the worker and the group have indeed set up the conditions for successful treatment. Successful completion of this stage is essential preparation to enter and cope with the tasks associated with the next stage of group development, namely power and control.

QUESTIONS FOR CONSIDERATION

1. What are some of the rituals associated with beginnings?

2. Identify some of the difficulties that may arise by inappropriate use of rituals.

3. What factors are likely to contribute to group members' anxiety during "pre-affiliation"?

4. What steps can the worker take to minimize anxiety in the group?

5. How might past experiences affect the group treatment process?

6. How will the client demonstrate ambivalence during pre-affiliation?

6

Worker Concerns and Intervention During Power and Control

It is imperative that the group go through and successfully complete the major tasks associated with the pre-affiliation stage of group development. Failure to do this will hinder or impede the group's progress at the *power and control* stage (Garland, Jones and Kolodny, 1965). Before beginning the major tasks associated with this stage, the worker should ensure that each member of the group understands and accepts a working agreement or contract based on the following:

- the worker's role in the group and his or her expectations of each member;
- each member's role in the group and their expectations of themselves and others;
- how concerns and issues will be discussed and handled in the group;
- the type and level of interaction and participation expected of each member;
- the principle of confidentiality and what personal issues are to be treated confidentially;
- when the group will begin and end each session and each members responsibility to attend sessions and be punctual;
- the treatment goals of each member and those of the group; and
- the role and expectations of the host organization.

The aforementioned list is not to imply a system of voting on each item, but rather a reaching of agreement through discussion, negotiation and compromise. The worker plays a critical role in this process, having a primary responsibility for ensuring that each member is clear about the contractual arrangement. If there is a lack of structure and an absence of clearly defined and accepted rules of behavior, the stage is set for the group to sabotage the treatment process.

With the contractual agreement, the worker and the group are ready to face the tasks associated with the power and control stage of the group system's development. Power and control is that stage of group development through which all treatment groups go as members begin to feel safer in their interactions with others. This state of safety and the beginnings of group identity usually lead members to test themselves in relation to others, including the worker. As members determine that the group is worth their emotional investment, issues of power and control emerge.

These issues are characterized by:

- attempts of group members to test themselves in relation to each other and to the worker;
- testing of emotional and psychological positions such as status, ranking, communication and choice making;
- testing of the worker's knowledge, skills and abilities in relation to authority and its use within the group;
- the formalizing of relationships and the creation of a hierarchy in the group (cliques and alliances);
- competition within the group; and
- the assumption and assigning of group roles.

Before any of these characteristics can be used to promote the treatment process, the worker should take into account the group member's stage of development with respect to their life cycle. As human beings mature they also go through clearly defined stages of development. Each stage is characterized by specific developmental tasks. If the clients are struggling with tasks related to achieving independence and autonomy, as is normal with adolescents, the power and control stage of group development will heighten the tensions and conflicts associated with this stage of group development.

Moreover, the worker can anticipate that many of the problems in a group for adolescents will revolve around issues of autonomy, independence, power and control. It would be reasonable to assume that most of the energies of this group will be concentrated in this stage of the group's development. However, since all human beings have some unresolved issues related to autonomy, independence, interdependence, power and control, all client groups will struggle with this stage of group development.

Testing of Self in Relation to Other Members and the Worker

As the operating structure of the group evolves, individual members cautiously test themselves in relation to each other. An example of this may be demonstrated by a member's preface at the beginning of sharing some personal information with the group: *I am not sure what you will think of me, but I will share my concerns with all of you.* This member would seem to be seeking the approval of the group for a particular disclosure. In fact, it may be a gesture to solicit from the group some statement of personal acceptance or liking. Another possible message from this member could be: *Is this a safe place to be, and to what extent is the worker competent, and will he or she protect me?* How the worker responds to this self-disclosure could influence the manner in which members relate to the worker as competent and helpful in the treatment process.

Such a preface offers the worker several options for intervention. Prior to making a specific intervention the worker should seek clarification of the meaning of the client's message in light of his or her maturational level and needs and how these needs may or may not be in keeping with group needs. The worker may reassure the member, and indeed the group, that he or she accepts and respects them as people. The worker should demonstrate this throughout the life of the group. The worker may indicate that the member's sharing is welcomed and use the sharing to stimulate self-examination through dialogue and discussion among members. The intervention may be designed to give support and encouragement to the specific member while modeling for the other members how to seek information from each other or how to respond to the needs of a member. Another purpose of the intervention may be to check the client's feelings and impressions about him or herself. In order to encourage participation and involvement in the treatment process, testing comments and statements should be clarified and understood by all group members. Such a process shows to the members that what they are saying is important and will be listened to by the worker and other members.

In a similar manner, members check the responses and reactions of the worker to see if their thoughts, emotions and behaviors are understood, accepted or rejected. The worker too should be sensitive to a member's reactions to his or her effect on the group. Until members are sure of themselves and the worker, and of their ability to follow the accepted rules of behavior of the group, there will be testing of each other. Such testing is a legitimate part of power and control.

Testing of Emotional and Psychological Positions

As members feel surer of their emotional and psychological positions, issues of status, ranking, communications, choice-making and influence arise. Members gradually begin to be themselves in the group situation. Some individuals dominate the discussion, or try to demonstrate their "superior" knowledge on the issues under discussion, while others may withdraw from involvement. For example, one member may, as a result of anxiety or to avoid exploration of his or her feelings, indicate to the group that the present experience is not unique to him or her and that he or she knows what will happen in the group.

Generally, communication patterns develop that indicate that individuals are seeking to establish a sphere of influence in the group. Members are often unsure of each other or the position they should take on the issues under discussion. The worker should be particularly sensitive to these patterns of communication, since they are likely to determine or support the tentative hypothesis that the worker has about each member. The issues here are ones of who has authority in the group and how will the worker demonstrate his or her authority. In a group for mothers of victims of sexual abuse, one mother made the following comment: *I have now gone through this kind of experience with two of my daughters and their father. I can write a book about the feelings you go through during these times.* For the worker, this response supported the notion that this member would set herself up as the authority on this subject. In a supportive and caring manner, the worker could help this member and the group examine the affective meaning of the statement and demonstrate how it could be used for the benefit of the group around authority issues. Moreover, strengths and weaknesses of each member may emerge as they seek to be themselves in the group. The worker's interventions should be directed toward helping the members struggle with their issues of autonomy, dependence and interdependence.

Testing a Worker's Knowledge, Skill and Competence

A normal part of human development is to move from a state of dependence on others toward one of interdependence with others, to challenge persons perceived to be in authority or control as we struggle for interdependence. In the group situation, this is most evident when members question the abilities of the worker. This is often done in an indirect manner. For example, a member may observe that in her last group experience she "did not feel safe ... ?" The underlying theme may be: What kind of leader are you? Will you be different from that worker?

Such a theme should not be ignored by the worker, but should be sensitively explored in order to identify the member's true feelings about the worker. It is also necessary to find out from the group how generalized is the concern regarding the worker's leadership abilities and skills. Understanding the stages of group development and the maturational level of the client group will help the worker to realize that a challenge to leadership is inevitable and should assist the worker in preparing to deal with this challenge effectively.

An effective response to this challenge would be for the worker to encourage the group members to openly discuss their feelings, thoughts, behaviors and their understanding of his or her role and leadership. In an orderly manner, the worker helps the members to focus on their reactions to his or her authority in particular and how these reactions are related or connected to similar experiences in their lives. Included in this discussion, it is likely that the worker's competence and adequacy as a leader and helper will arise. Questions of competence and adequacy are likely to be disturbing for the worker if he or she is not expecting them. These questions may also raise issues of authority for the worker and how his or her authority can be used. This situation may create anxiety if the worker has unresolved issues around authority or fears of losing control of the group. The challenge could be used to demonstrate how to deal with a difficult situation and promote change; or to punish members who challenge the worker's authority, with the result that feelings about authority are submerged and the treatment process severely undermined.

As was noted earlier, testing of the worker is inevitable during this stage. The only effective tool available to the worker is the contractual agreement that was earlier developed between all members and the worker. A skillful intervention would be for the worker, sensing a possible impasse around power and control issues, to ask the group to examine how the present discussion or activity will help individuals and the group as a whole to achieve their stated goals and objectives. For example, a group of perpetrators of sexual abuse on young children have spent the last half hour arguing about the unfairness of the justice system. Three members of the group became very loud in their efforts to shout each other down. One member, Tom, turned to the worker and asked: *Why don't you decide which of us is right?*

Worker: *How would my ruling on the present issue help us to achieve the things we have agreed to work on together, namely, accepting responsibilities for your actions with your children, changing your behaviors in this area, and how you can rebuild a supportive and caring home environment for you and your family?*

The group responded with what seemed like a long silence, which was broken by Tom, who said: *By having this discussion, I have been avoiding looking at my responsibility for my behavior with my son. I am ashamed of what I have done.* Without a clear statement of agreed upon goals and objectives, the worker is impotent in the task of leading the group through its power-and-control phase of development.

Formalizing of Relationships

As members become more comfortable in the group they begin to formalize their relationships and create a hierarchy within the group. For example, some persons talk more than others; other persons seem almost automatically to fall into the follower role; others play mediating roles; some play the role of clarifier of questions and issues; and still others seem to be the barometer for assessing where the group is at any given time. In such a situation the formation of cliques and alliances is inevitable.

As cliques and alliances form, it is very likely that scapegoating will occur. Members who appear to be weaker or who appear to be exceptionally strong may be scapegoated by the majority of the group. This is a means through which the group may exclude or use some members for reasons that are often not clear to them. The worker's role in this situation is to encourage the member or members who have been scapegoated to examine the feelings connected with being scapegoated and conversely to have the persons scapegoating, look at their feelings as they use the scapegoating technique. It is very likely that in the context of the treatment group those members who are different or deviant in any way will be readily scapegoated. It is also inevitable that persons will begin to act out their normal life scripts during this period of interaction.

A student social worker, assigned to the student counseling services department in a university setting, observed that whenever there was conflict and tension in a group of students who were working on issues of trust and close relationships, two students seemed to be the target of the other students' anger. The student worker asked all members to examine their feelings and behaviors toward each other and if there were other times when similar feelings and behaviors occurred. *Yes, replied one of the students, I can't stand tension and conflict. I have always tried to find an immediate solution for the situation, much to the annoyance and anger of my family and my peers. I want to understand what I do. I would like some feedback from all of you.* To be fully helpful to any treatment group in a similar situation, the worker must be aware of the life scripts of members and how these can be used as part of the change process.

It would be very easy for the worker to diffuse any signs of potential conflict or potential scapegoating. To do so is to indicate to members that the worker is uncomfortable handling strong feelings or difficult situations and to model for them that such situations will not be tolerated. Through the skillful use of the contract the worker ought to clear with the group what agreements they have made in relation to the tasks to be accomplished, and examine critically why such an agreement does or does not work, and to what extent the individual members want to commit themselves to accomplishing the primary purpose of the group–treatment. All of the above should be done in the context of problem solving–identifying the problem, getting supporting data in relation to the problem, assessing that data, looking at the options and their attendant consequences, and then helping members decide which option would be most appropriate for them to accomplish their treatment goals. Unless the issues that arise during the power and control phase are dealt with in an orderly and sequential manner, it is likely that confusion will ensue and that members may withdraw both physically and emotionally from further interaction with the group. On the other hand, it is to the advantage of the group for the worker to demonstrate that conflict can be constructive and to model for the members how the contract can be used as a means of re-negotiating positions and highlighting for the group the competence and adequacy of the worker to help the group accomplish the task to which it is committed.

Summary

The stage of power and control is frequently the most difficult for the beginning practitioner. It brings to the fore the worker's issues around authority and how authority can be used. Human beings never resolve completely the issues of authority. It is essential that the worker have a clear sense of purpose in relation to the group as a whole and in this phase in particular, so that he or she may be able to communicate to the group the use of authority as a problem-solving tool. The worker should be prepared for the group to question, attack and challenge his or her ability to lead. The response should not be a defensive one, but rather it should be one of understanding, with a commitment to use the group to demonstrate the need for rules and agreements on the tasks and the accomplishment of those tasks.

As the worker reminds the group of its tasks, its rules and agreements and probably how well the members have functioned before, it can be expected that at a subconscious level, several members may be upset with the worker's prodding. This is a normal response to authority and in this context the worker is demonstrating his or her authority to the group. By examining this situation in a problem-solving manner, the worker may help the group to explore other times when members had similar reactions to the ones they presently have and, with the group, decide if the feelings and behaviors are problematic for them, and if so explore ways through which specific changes may occur.

As the group resolves its difficulties around power and control with the skillful use of the contract by the worker or other member, the group finds itself in a psychological state that helps it move beyond the issues of power and control to issues of intimacy. There is a new sense of cohesion and be-longing in the group and frequently a commitment to the purposes and objectives to which the group has agreed. This is often accompanied by ex-hilaration and a feeling that no task is impossible for the group to accomplish. It also places the worker firmly in the authority position with members accepting that authority as legitimate while seeking the support and leadership of other members.

QUESTIONS FOR CONSIDERATION

1. What characteristics would indicate that the group is in the power and control stage of its development?

2. What are the issues and concerns that clients face during this stage of group development?

3. How can the worker help the group to resolve authority issues during this stage?

4. How can the worker use his knowledge of life cycle development during power and control?

5. What are the group characteristics that a worker can expect during this group stage?

6. Why is contracting important during power and control?

7. In what ways would failure to complete the tasks of the pre-affiliation stage create difficulty during the power and control stage?

7

Worker Concerns and Intervention During Intimacy

As mentioned earlier, no stage of group development is discrete. All groups move through stages during their existence with many of the stages constantly overlapping. If the group has successfully developed a clear understanding of the treatment tasks to be accomplished, and how it will proceed with these tasks, then the group is considered to have completed the power and control stage of its development. This is not to say that power and control issues will not arise later in the group's life.

This accomplishment leads the group to the point where there is structure. The group has established rules, norms and roles for the members including the worker and cohesion and group feeling is beginning. This structure provides the group with a sense of safety and trust, even through there may be some discomfort for the individual member. Ideally, the worker used interventions that demonstrated competence so that members now have confidence in the worker's ability to help the group accomplish its treatment goals.

This confidence is based on the worker's ability to intervene appropriately, to clarify issues, interpret and confront sensitively (respecting members' feelings) and monitor the workings of the group and its members. It is crucial that the worker acknowledge member contributions, especially affective ones, and give positive feedback.

Against such a background, the group is able to move into the third stage of group development known as *intimacy*. In this stage the relationships among members are more intimate and less formal than during pre-affiliation and power and control. It is conceivable that some members may still be at the power and control stage, but the pervading feelings and attitudes of the group in general, are those of intimacy or belonging.

The stage of intimacy is characterized by the clearly identifiable elements of:

- a pseudo-sense of security,
- a sense of cohesion,

- strong feelings of ambivalence about the group,
- regression, and
- the re-enactment of family dynamics.

In addition to recognizing the above elements, the worker, in order to be most helpful to the group, must understand the group as an interacting social system, must understand how family systems operate and the relevance of this knowledge to the treatment group. During this stage the group is a dynamic entity with clear boundaries that help members to perceive and feel the group as unique, special and important. Underlying this stage is a beginning sense of trust among the members and the worker.

A Pseudo-Sense of Security

The security that members feel in the group at the beginning of this stage is often more imaginary than real. This feeling flows from the members' perception of the group as a real entity, with shared tasks to be accomplished and a direction on how to proceed with them. This security is often shattered in the group. For example, one member may unwittingly test the security and trust in the group by sharing very personal information, by challenging the expressed opinions of another member, or by asking the group to discuss or give advice on a sensitive or controversial issue. In any of these situations members may feel threatened emotionally. If so, they will react characteristically by withdrawing from participation in the group, or by verbally lashing out at the member or the group. In a couples group one member, Mary, made the statement: *We have not enjoyed sexual intercourse for several years now. It is important to me. I will not continue like this!* The group became very silent, with members avoiding eye contact with each other. Finally, another member, Jane, said: *You should never discuss such matters outside of your bedroom. I don't like it and I feel very uncomfortable here. If this is what you want to talk about, I will not return to the group.*

Such a scenario could readily lead members to perceive the group as unsafe and question why the group should exist at all. Recognizing that the group's sense of security is threatened, the worker should be prepared to help the group examine its present dilemma in a problem-solving manner, and then evaluate the present situation with respect to the treatment goals and the agreed upon group contract. This strategy restores confidence in the group and its ability to meet its treatment goals and objectives: thus assuring members that their investment in the group is warranted. Members would also have had an opportunity to use problem-solving skills to cope with a real crisis. By using his understanding of human interaction, the worker may respond as follows: *I sense some discomfort as you talk about sexual matters here. That is understandable. But, could we look at what feelings and thoughts were raised for you when Mary said what she said.*

Sense of Cohesion

The appearance of group cohesion during this stage of development emerges after the group has successfully dealt with painful and uncomfortable experiences. Corey and Corey (1982) note that if a group chooses to remain comfortable or to stick with superficial interactions, then there will be little group togetherness (p. 152).

Facing the difficulties of beginning and the struggles related to power and control, often provide the group with affective rationales for wanting to be close. The evidence of group cohesion indicates to the worker that members can now be encouraged to deepen their level of risk-taking, caring and sharing. The concept of interdependence and the need for mutual support and responsibility should be stressed and encouraged. Group cohesion gives support to members going through difficult situations both within and outside of the group, while providing a supportive environment in which members and the worker can challenge and confront each other in order to achieve the treatment goals and objectives. For example, a member of a group may verbalize his or her difficulty in sharing personal content, to find that most members have the same difficulty and that all members are interested and willing to be helpful. Members may indicate that they feel good enough about the group to share information that they have not shared previously. The development and manifestation of cohesion in the treatment group are critical to the group's survival. The group is perceived by its members during this stage as being a special place with special people to which they belong. Such a perception encourages participation and commitment.

With this sense of togetherness, the content of members' presentations becomes much more personal and less censored. The themes presented at this time usually revolve around relationship issues such as trust, adequacy/inadequacy, dependence/independence, feelings of low self-esteem and the myriad of feelings, thoughts and behaviors related to these issues. Several affective themes seem to arise for discussion at the same time. The worker's task is to help members to identify the many themes presented, prioritize them and then systematically explore the chosen themes. It is unlikely that all of the identified themes can or will be discussed during the life of the group. The emphasis should be on members developing problem-solving skills in relation to their life situations, rather than exploring each theme. For example, in a group for mothers of sexually abused children, one mother shares with the group that since she learned of the abusive situation she has been unable to have a close, intimate relationship with her husband. To this another mother responds, in tears: *I have wanted to castrate my spouse. My daughter's experience reminds me of what my own father did to me many years ago.* This example highlights several things, namely, the sharing of very personal and painful material with the group; the provision of support through sharing and the presentation of several themes that need to be addressed by the group. Some of these themes are: fear of having close relationships with men; guilt for feeling anger; unresolved conflicts about past experiences and situations; ambivalence about authority and poor self image, to mention a few. Sometimes another member will identify the themes and the pain of other members. Failing that, the worker may help the group members to explore the relevance of the earlier statements to themselves and help them decide which themes they want to pursue. Frequently, such statements are made near the end of a group session. Should this occur, the worker should help the member and the group to decide how important are the issues raised and let the member or the group take responsibility for raising these issues again at later sessions.

During intimacy, the defenses of members are considerably lower. This lowering of defenses should be carefully assessed and monitored by the worker to ensure that members do not become overly vulnerable to each other by making statements and comments they may later regret or that may be misused by others. If the group is functioning well at this stage, the worker should play a less dominant role than during the "pre-affiliation" and "termination" stages of the group. Members should be taking most of the responsibility for managing the group.

Feelings of Ambivalence

Another recognizable element of intimacy is ambivalence. Unlike the initial ambivalence regarding the members' concerns about being in the group, the ambivalence now centers on such questions as: *How much do I disclose in this group? Should I disclose? What are the dangers or "pay-offs" for me? How close should I be to others? How much distance should I maintain? Will I be safe in this group or will I give more than I plan to?*

Feelings of ambivalence during intimacy are usually reflected in such statements as: *I am learning a lot about my interactions with others but I don't know how long I can tolerate the pain;* or: *This is a great experience with terrific people, but I always feel so naked in this group;* or: *I am afraid of the closeness I feel to this group. I may have to back away from some of you. I need some distance.* While acknowledging the group experience as good or helpful, members may still articulate their discomfort and ambivalence, in relation to each other and the treatment process. Members may emotionally, psychologically and sometimes physically withdraw in order to gain some sense of security and to feel less vulnerable in the presence of others.

As the worker observes these feelings of ambivalence, the group should be helped to understand that such feelings are normal when members are faced with change. The ambivalence could then be explored in a problem-solving manner, with emphasis on discussing the positive and negative aspects to change. In this context the worker would support and encourage all behaviors that help members to move toward their change goals and objectives. Personal change is difficult to contemplate and bring about. However, a cohesive, supportive group treatment environment can facilitate such changes. Worker interventions should be geared to creating such an environment.

Regression

Withdrawal by individual members or the entire group from involvement could be interpreted as regression. Members will react in this characteristic manner when they feel threatened or vulnerable. Some members may withdraw from the group activity or discussion; some may try to intellectualize their feelings and behavior, and even the feelings and behavior of others; and others may be critical of themselves and other members. If unchallenged, any or all these regressive postures could effectively sabotage the group's performance in relation to the treatment tasks.

Sometimes the challenge comes from a member of the group. The challenge could be confrontational and may further alienate members of the group. However, if attention is drawn to the impact of the regressive behavior on the group by either member or worker, the group is helped to use the regressive behavior constructively. For example, a group of teenagers has been meeting for the last six weeks at a settlement house to discuss their problems with drug abuse. The last two sessions have been characterized by feelings of closeness and sincere sharing. At this particular meeting Sam informs the group that he saw another member, Brenda, talking with his mother earlier that day. Sam accused Brenda of telling his mother about his involvement with drugs, even though he acknowledged that his mother did not tell him what she and Brenda were talking about. The impact on the group is devastating. Several members shout accusations at each other about breaking trust and confidentiality. With the support of the worker, a group member asks the group to listen for a minute. He or she then recounts the successes they have achieved individually and collectively and then challenges members to look at what could be learned from their present situation. The results are immediate. Members begin to share their fears of being caught with drugs by their parents, school authorities and the police. In this way the regressive behaviors are used constructively by the group.

The Re-Enactment of Family Dynamics

The above elements of intimacy lead the worker to perceive the group as having many of the characteristics of a family system. Members of the group assume and play out the characteristic roles of a family. For example, one member may try to mediate between members; another may play the role of clown in order to introduce levity and thus hinder serious discussion; another, in conjunction with the worker, may function as the group's authority figure on many matters; one may be the quiet member of the group; yet another may act out to protect the group from having to look at its processes and problems. In other words, members begin to act out their life scripts as they have done in their families.

This aspect of intimacy offers the worker one of the major therapeutic tools of the group treatment process. The worker can use an understanding of family dynamics to develop some perspective on the roles that members traditionally play in their actual families, and their current family arrangements, their strengths and weaknesses in such roles and so help them to understand how past influences may operate in the group situation. In this way, members could be made aware of their individual treatment goals and also the treatment goals of the group. A member of a group may gain some insight into the role he may be playing in the group—for instance, that of mediator in every disagreement or situation of tension or conflict in the group. Some reflection by the member with the support of other members may help this particular member to explain: *I have always played this role in my family and it has been difficult, since I never seem to have anyone address my needs.* This statement opens the door for the worker and other members to examine with each other how the roles members are currently playing out are similar or like the roles they acted out in their actual families. Such insights can be used to encourage members to identify the roles and interactions they want to change during the treatment process with the assistance of the group.

Another treatment intervention open to the worker is that of helping the group and the individual members examine their world view, their ways of interacting and their manner of behavior. The change process could then be implemented to bring consistency between the positions of the group and the member in these three areas. The principal role of the worker during intimacy is to help the group to maintain focus on the treatment tasks in spite of the occurring change and discomfort, and to give positive feedback to members when they risk themselves in the group. In addition, should the group become bogged down in the achievement of its treatment tasks the worker may remind the group of its earlier commitment to the tasks. If there is no clear statement of the contract and the treatment goals for the individual and the group, there can be no clear assessment of the work that has been done and that still needs to be done.

Intimacy then, is characterized by an increasing intensity of the relationships among the various members of the group. This intensification allows members to challenge each other, to show more vulnerability, to be more supportive of each other and frequently to look for support or approval.

Garland, Jones and Kolodny (1965), in their articulation of these stages of group development, indicate that the frame of reference for this phase could be seen as the family. It is easy for individuals to reflect on what their own family experiences have been and to relate present behaviors and affective responses to that background. The family, then, provides a useful framework.

Summary

As members get to know each other in a more intimate context they feel more comfortable about allowing their true selves to show. This opening up allows the worker to identify some of the issues and concerns that may be problematic and that need to be addressed in the treatment context. Such issues revolve around authority, the expression of feelings in relation to one's self and others, sharing, participation in discussion, group interaction and the ability to be close and intimate.

As the group goes through intimacy, the issues and topics discussed take on a more personal character. Members may talk about their feelings for another person; about their sexuality; about their fears of closeness; their concerns about relating to specific persons; and about their prejudices. There is a greater willingness to risk self revelation. Many of these personal issues will be raised but cannot all be discussed at the same time. It is for the worker to help the group determine what issues are important to the group and to help them to put the issues in the context of the treatment purpose and decide, in a systematic and orderly manner, how the issues will be dealt with. The problem-solving approach should be used. The discussion should be organized around the identification of the issue, its various aspects, the supporting data (whether that data be behavioral, cognitive, affective, or combinations of these), an assessment of the data presented, an examination of the possible options for the members in relation to their specific goals and objectives, and then the choosing of one of the options with a built-in monitoring feed-back mechanism that will allow the individual and the group to evaluate the chosen option. An objective for the worker is to help the members to organize their thinking in an orderly fashion and to demonstrate their ability to implement whatever plans or commitments they make to their fellow members.

It is likely that during this phase members will demonstrate more emotion than during earlier stages. Some of the issues that members of the group are dealing with may also be issues for the worker. The worker, therefore, has a responsibility to recognize this, but that this is not the place to deal with such issues. The worker's role at this time is to help the group deal with its issues and concerns in a constructive and healthy manner. Failure to do so may cause the worker to block some areas of discussion because of personal discomfort and so create the potential for a dysfunctional group. The possibility of being stuck in this phase due to the lack of self-awareness becomes very real, and the benefit of the treatment process may be minimized for several or all members of the group. For example, the worker may have some difficulty around the issue of closeness with others. As the group members explore developing closer relationships among each other, the worker may subconsciously attempt to refocus the discussion in order to avoid the personal pain incurred by close relationships. This lack of self awareness by the worker is often justified as being in the best interest of the group and its members.

The successful completion of this stage gives the individual member a better sense of self, a better sense of self in relation to others, and a better ability to assess his or her life and its options. It can be an opportunity for members to test each other in matters that are of a very personal and intensely emotional nature. The primary task for the worker during this stage of development is to be supportive and to encourage the sharing of the appropriate personal data. Because the group is able to successfully problem-solve during this phase of intimacy, it will experience a new sense of cohesion and togetherness that will facilitate the treatment process, and allow members to raise issues that for them might have been too personal to share earlier.

QUESTIONS FOR CONSIDERATION

1. No stage of group development is discrete in practice. What characteristics of group development surface during intimacy?

2. How is an understanding of family dynamics helpful to the worker during the intimacy stage of group development?

3. What factors are likely to jeopardize a feeling of cohesion during intimacy?

4. What interventions can the worker use as therapeutic tools during the stage of intimacy?

8

Worker Concerns and Intervention During Differentiation

Aspects of the predominant stage in which the group is working will readily come to the fore soon after each group session begins. If the group is in the stage of *differentiation*, the session will begin showing aspects of pre-affiliation, power and control and intimacy. As each session ends, aspects of termination will be evident. During each session, the treatment group goes through the five recognizable stages of development. One of these stages is differentiation.

In order to assist the group with its treatment tasks, the worker must recognize and utilize the various characteristics of the stage of differentiation, which are that:

- the differences and uniqueness of members begin to emerge;
- members begin to perceive the worker as a real person and not as super-human;
- members begin to accept each other and themselves as unique individuals;
- positive, realistic and constructive feedback occurs;
- mutual support and self-help are evident;
- members become ambivalent regarding their change process;
- new behaviors are tested;
- members sensitively challenge each other to make changes in their lives; and
- members accept and use the problem-solving method to confront their life situations.

All of the elements listed derive from the cohesion and sense of belonging that develops during the earlier stages of the group's development. As members work through their issues and concerns regarding authority, their present roles and statuses in the group, how these roles may have been fashioned in their families of origin and how they express affect, members are helped to recognize their many differences in relation to one another and to see themselves and each other as unique individuals.

Differences and Uniqueness

As the group moves through differentiation, which is often referred to as the working stage of the group, members perceive and verbalize their similarities, their differences and their uniqueness in relation to others. As noted, the group is now functioning in an intimate and cohesive manner. Incorporated in this way of functioning are many of the dynamics and tensions that are observed in family functioning. In families, the experiences, sense of caring and sense of belonging, help members of the family to recognize the differences between and among family members. Similarly, in the group treatment context, members usually are able to recognize how they are different from each other. In spite of the differences and the uniqueness of each person, the members learn to communicate in the group and show that they care and respect each other. For example, Ann, a member of a group of separated parents, shared with the group that in order to gain some influence over her ex-spouse, she used their children as pawns in her bargaining with him for additional support payments. To this, John, another group member responded: *I like and admire you very much, but I don't understand how you could do this. I guess we do what we have to do. However, I wish you would use a different method for getting increased support from your ex*. This example indicates that John is now able to be critical of Ann's behavior while being positive in his feelings about her as a person. He is able to push her in the direction of looking at and possibly changing her behavior.

The role of the worker in this context is to help members identify the similarities that bind the group together yet be aware of and accept that there are different perceptions, attitudes, values, behaviors and feelings. Moreover, in spite of the many differences each member can be encouraged to make his or her own unique contribution to the group in general and to the achievement of individual treatment goals. It is through the unique contributions of individuals that members gain personal insights into their own situations. With the awareness gained, members can be challenged by each other and the worker to change their ways of thinking, feeling and behaving. This is the essence of the group treatment process.

Perceptions of the Worker as a Real Person

As a result of the shared experiences of the group, particularly as the worker models acceptance of members, gives them positive feedback for sharing and risk taking, and discloses selected aspects of feeling and thinking that are similar to those of the members, the worker is seen as a real person and not as a super-human being. For example, in a group situation, the worker shares his or her fears about not being a perfect parent. To this, several members responded that until she told them of this they saw her as super-human, someone who did not make mistakes. Now they saw the worker as a trained professional who shared and could identify with some of their issues and concerns.

Such insight helps members in their efforts to develop their own identity rather than struggle to be just like the worker. One of the goals of treatment is for members to accept themselves as they are and use their strengths and resources to be the best they can be, rather than try to be someone else, including the worker. Seeing the worker as real demystifies the treatment process and helps members to recognize that the problems and concerns they bring can be resolved by their active involvement in treatment. The worker is part of a shared experience with specific group treatment skills. During this stage the worker promotes the perception of realness, the orderly and conscious use of the problem-solving sequence, and the appropriate use of self-disclosure in order to facilitate member insight and awareness.

Climate of Acceptance and Support

As the group perceives the worker as a real, fallible person facing similar issues that they themselves face, its members also recognize that the treatment tasks can only be accomplished through their efforts and involvement. With this recognition and the worker's modeling, members learn to accept and support each other. Members indicate to each other that they understand the struggles and issues that they face while giving encouragement. During this stage members frequently demonstrate their caring for each other and are able to offer constructive suggestions based on their own life experiences.

In such a climate, there is the further development of mutual support and self-help. Members verbalize that they are in this together and together can help each other. Cohesion among members is at its highest and there is a sense of comradeship and commitment to the common purpose of achieving the treatment tasks of each member and of the group. The worker's role in such a situation is to support and encourage the sense of community that exists and at the same time to challenge members to try new measures to achieve their stated goals and objectives. The worker can expect that the discussion or activity during this stage would revolve around the themes of identity and interdependence.

Ambivalence Regarding the Change Process

As the group works through differentiation, members are challenged to achieve their treatment goals. These challenges are often met with resistance. Such resistance should not necessarily be interpreted as un-healthy. When confronted with the need for change all human beings tend to shy away from changing, even though recognizing the need to change.

Ambivalence toward change is a normal human response. Although group members in the earlier stages of the group contracted to pursue spe-cific treatment goals, when the costs of change are assessed by members, they may seem too high. The worker's role in the group at this time, is to help members to normalize their feelings of ambivalence regarding the proposed change, then to realistically evaluate the advantages and disad-vantages of the change and to take action in keeping with their treatment goals. For example, a group of foster parents in a child welfare setting iden-tified one of their treatment goals as wanting to respond differently to the foster children in their care when these children swore at them when repri-manded. During a session characterized predominantly by elements of differentiation one parent observed: *I know I should not retaliate by screaming at Janet, since my screaming seems to encourage her to continue swearing at me. My own children never swore at me. But screaming has always worked with my children and my other foster children. Why should I change?* To this, members of the group and the worker indicated that they understood what this member was feeling. One member said: *It's like you want to and yet you don't want to be different with Janet. What is the worst that could happen if you were different?* This example highlights member-member support in the group and a member's attempt to help a peer deal with her ambivalence toward change by forcing the parent to come to terms with her fears about the proposed change. What is the worst that could happen? The worker could support the mem-ber-member interaction with positive comments and help the group to see the implications of this example for personal change.

Testing of New Behavior

At this stage members have become aware of the impact of their families of origin in molding and shaping their affective, cognitive and behavioral functioning, and often recognize that the roles in which they function best are not always ideal in many other social interactions. The group situation highlights for many members, through dynamic interaction, many of the shortcomings of their normal functioning. For example, in a group, one member may have been helped to see that during his or her interactions with others, contradictory verbal and non-verbal messages were given. This member's treatment goal may be to gain some congruency between his verbal and non-verbal presentations. The group at this time is likely to confront the member whenever double messages are given. Other mem-bers and the worker, in an environment of safety, if not comfort, may encourage the member to try new ways of relating, in order to minimize the incongruence. As the member tries out new behaviors while relating, other members are quick to give honest and realistic feedback in a sensitive and caring manner. Members can be taught to challenge other members whose feedback is overly critical and given in an uncaring manner, because when the feedback is given in a sensitive and helpful manner, individuals are able to accept it and this in turn will reinforce the desired behaviors. In this way, the individual's treatment goals may be achieved with group support. The group is therefore achieving one of its primary objectives, namely individual change through the group process.

Sensitive Challenging of Members

Not only is the member encouraged to try new behaviors in the group, but members are encouraged by each other and the worker to take their insights and learning from the microcosm of the group into the macrocosm of their larger social environments. The group provides a forum for members to make connections between what is going on in the group and what is going on in their lives outside of the group. During differentiation the worker and the group constantly challenge members to change—to try new ways of doing things and to share the results of the changes. Members are supported in their struggles to find new systems and methods of interacting.

The worker models for the group in a sensitive manner how these challenges for change may be initiated. For example, the worker may say to a member: *I can feel your struggle to do things differently. Could you tell us how we may be helpful to you?* In this way, the worker is indicating that he or she is listening to the member and wants to be helpful and supportive. Such an approach encourages members to verbalize their fears and concerns about change and gives other members the opportunity to be supportive.

Acceptance and Use of the Problem-Solving Sequence

As the group, moves through its stages of development, the worker helps members to see the relevance and effectiveness of the problem-solving method. Whenever the group is inclined to lose its sense of purpose or focus, another member or the worker may bring this problem to its attention. In such a manner, this response by a member reinforces for each member an appreciation and understanding of the problem-solving sequence and how it can help them to deal effectively with their concerns.

As members confront their life situations, in and out of the group, they learn to use the problem-solving sequence—namely, to identify the issue, concern or problem; to provide the supporting affective, cognitive and behavioral data; to assess the data; to examine and evaluate the options; to choose an option; to implement it and evaluate the outcomes. Only with a sound grasp of this process will members learn to take responsibility for their lives.

During differentiation the worker uses the understanding of life cycle development to predict issues that are likely to arise. The level of maturity of the members will influence how effectively the problem-solving method can be used.

The worker's primary task is to assist with the clarification and interpretation of the process as it unfolds. By this time members have learned their various roles and will be performing these key functions for the group. The worker can be helpful to the members through self-disclosure in ways that would help to clarify or intensify a particular experience for them. This self-disclosure by the worker encourages a sense of cohesion and belonging. The members will be feeling a sense of ownership of the group—that it is their group constituted for them in order to accomplish their goals.

During this stage the group attempts to maintain the sense of intimacy and caring that developed during an earlier stage of its development. However, rather than expect or look for the support of the worker to encourage this intimacy, individual members take more responsibility for encouraging each other to maintain and achieve a deeper level of caring. Members are encouraged to examine all aspects of their social and personal relationships and at the same time look at other relationships outside of the group. There must be support and encouragement for trying new behaviors outside of the group and seeking the group's response to these efforts after they have been tried—not only new behaviors but also new patterns of thinking and feeling. Such support and encouragement serves to heighten constructive criticism between and among members. In order to better understand this stage of development, it is useful to review the analogy of the adolescent who seems to be dependent on his family yet finds a very strong push to be different from them and to leave home. The adolescent goes through a stage of trying to be independent until he recognizes that there are consequences to independence and that interdependence is the ideal to be sought after. So too, in the group, individuals know that they are all in this experience for their own benefit but learn that they need each other to achieve their individual and group goals.

The treatment situation will be influenced by earlier group experiences of members. Members acknowledge whether the experience has helped them more than previous experiences or whether the experience is similar to earlier experiences that they found difficult. Members recognize their interdependence within the group and the concept of mutual aid and support becomes of paramount importance. If the worker has been modeling adequately for the group he or she will be minimally involved at the differentiation stage and there is likely to be little, if any, evidence of conflict. Members will have learned how to communicate their feelings, their attitudes, their thoughts and their behaviors without conflict. However, if conflict does occur, as it does in all social systems, the conflict should be put in a realistic perspective, with members trying to separate the facts from feelings using a critical problem-solving mode that should lead to satisfactory resolution. Throughout this stage there is a consolidation of the various aspects of the treatment process for the individual and the group. Closeness emerges yet it is balanced by member differences. This closeness is to be encouraged.

As part of this stage, good communication patterns develop between members. Challenge is counter-balanced by support. Clarifications are sought and are often readily given. Group cohesion, empathy and caring are high, yet appropriate. The worker, even though essential throughout the treatment process, is less central during this stage than at any other. The group can now take on increased responsibilities for itself. Individual members are clear about the treatment tasks and are more ready to share feelings and thoughts. Game playing is likely to be at a minimum. There is an effort to communicate honestly and freely and even though the content may appear to be heavy, it is not overwhelming. The support within the group allows members to deal with such content realistically and honestly. Often, during this stage, there is excitement about personal achievements and about the achievements of others. Interdependence is highlighted, while dependence is minimized. There is a need to see others as they are and to accept their uniqueness.

Throughout this stage, strong interpersonal and group bonds develop where members feel a sense of ownership about all aspects of the group's life. In many situations they feel that everything in the environment ought to be brought into their microcosmic social system.

Among the stages of group development this stage has the greatest potential for individual change. Our earlier thesis is that the purpose of the group is individual treatment and by individual treatment we mean positive individual change in behavior, attitudes and feelings or combinations of these. The support and empathy from members of the group encourages all members to examine their areas of concern and make efforts to correct the areas of dysfunction in their lives.

QUESTIONS FOR CONSIDERATION

1. What are the major characteristics of the stage of differentiation?

2. How are these different from the previous stage of intimacy?

3. How do these characteristics affect the role of the worker?

4. In what ways can the worker use an understanding of this stage to promote positive change in the members?

9

Worker Concerns and Intervention During Separation

The final stage of group development is referred to as *separation*. This stage should not suddenly occur for the group, but should have been discussed as part of the group's contract during the beginning phase of the group. The group goes through separation as it ends each session. Successful separation is as critical to the group members as is pre-affiliation. A good experience with separation will reinforce the gains of earlier stages and assist members as they face new beginnings throughout their lives.

As the group moves toward the end of its agreed-upon number of sessions, the worker helps members to systematically examine and discuss the issues and concerns related to this ending. Regardless of when the matter of separation is raised, there are always difficulties for members and workers alike. It must be borne in mind that for all human beings, separation is symbolic of the ultimate end that comes for each of us, namely death. Separation must be recognized and dealt with at the beginning of the group process so that the group will be given the time and the opportunity to deal with the many issues and concerns that are associated with this particular ending.

The worker and each group member are predisposed to handle separation in his or her own unique manner. To grasp the various ways that human beings deal with issues of separation, the following scenario may be useful. A very close friend or relative comes to visit for a weekend. Their scheduled time of departure is Monday morning by the 7:30 train. Each person will handle the departure of their loved-one in his or her own unique manner. The options are many. A few of these are:

- on Sunday evening discuss the visit, its importance, and arrangements for getting to the train next morning;
- not to even mention the visit but to make plans for getting to the train;
- at bedtime on Sunday evening to indicate that you will not be available to go to the train station but have made arrangements for the loved-one to get there;

- to discuss the visit, the arrangements for departure and future contacts;
- not to mention the visit or any arrangements to leave;
- to make elaborate plans for breakfast on Monday morning and specific times and arrangements for getting to the station;
- to find activity and discussion to fill in the time prior to the loved-one's departure;
- to reminisce about earlier shared experiences; or
- to deny that the visit will be over shortly.

If we choose to take our visitor to the train station, some of us will leave our visitor outside the station with his or her bags and hurry off. Others will enter the station and chat for awhile. Yet others will go on to the platform and wave goodbye long after the train is out of sight, even though unable to see where the visitor is sitting. All of the above will be accompanied by a variety of emotional states such as happiness, sadness, relief, mild forms of depression and possibly excitement about future visits.

If the purpose of the group is clear; if goals and objectives have been clearly stated, internalized and worked on, then separation can be a very rewarding and satisfying experience. It is essential then, that the worker recognize the principal characteristics of this stage of the treatment process. During separation, the themes raised and discussed are characterized by:

- flight
- denial
- regression
- a need to continue
- recapitulation
- review and evaluation

(Garland, Jones and Kolodny, 1965)

Flight

As the group works through its separation stage, members will display two types of flight patterns as a way of dealing with the pain associated with ending or loss. One pattern shows members as denying the value of the group experience, sometimes aggressively attacking other members and the worker for not making the experience a significant one for them. Others may miss some sessions or all of the sessions where issues related to separation are discussed. The second pattern of flight is evidenced when members report that even though the group is still very important in their lives, they are developing other interests and activities outside the group. This development is positive and should be supported by the worker. For example, in a group for persons who have recently experienced the loss of a significant relationship, in an effort to control his pain and suffering at the separation of the group one member made the following comments: *I have gained nothing from these group sessions. I feel cheated. You have not responded to my pain and I don't think I will attend the remaining sessions.* The impact of this statement on the group was devastating. Other members tried to indicate to the member that they cared, and that they thought the group had been helpful to everyone. But it is likely that this member might not return to the group, and if he did, that he would negatively affect the other members.

An option open to the worker is to help the individual reframe the issue of rejection and the lack of caring into that of a response to loss, namely the loss of the group. In a problem-solving manner, the members could discuss and even demonstrate their feelings around the loss, explore other occasions and situations when similar feelings were experienced, review how the earlier situations were resolved, the options available to resolve this and other situations of loss. They could also look at how the members might make this situation different from earlier ones. In this way, flight provides a strong stimulus for changing a member's dysfunctional separation behaviors. Rather than emotionally and physically leaving the group, which is likely to engender feelings of dissatisfaction and incompleteness (unfinished business), the member is helped to accept the feelings as normal and understandable. Fleeing from stressful situations does not in itself resolve the affect related to the situation.

The other aspect of flight is readily seen in the following example. Six sessions before a long-term treatment group for substance abusers was due to end, several members of the group announced that they had begun new relationships with persons outside the drug culture. One member observed: *For the past two weeks I have been busy every evening. I have joined a fitness club, a discussion group and a bridge club. These new friends are nearly as important to me as you are.* Such a statement should be supported by the worker and the group. In fact, the worker may use this information to see if other members are developing support networks outside of the group. The member could be asked to tell how the initial contacts outside the group were developed and to discuss their advantages and disadvantages. Other members may then be encouraged to use this member's experience as a model to initiate outside contacts and interests.

Denial

Denial is a defense mechanism that we use in an attempt to block out painful situations or events. After members of the group have developed cohesion and togetherness, and most members have achieved their treatment goals and objectives, the group must face the reality of disbanding. As members face the loss of the group, it is easy for them to remember other painful situations of loss. To deal with this pain, members often deny that the group is ending at the given time and may interact with each other as though this reality was not imminent or inevitable. For example, as the worker or a group member reminds the group that their last session is only a few weeks away, the response of several members of a couples group was: *I don't remember us agreeing to end at a particular time. I thought that we would continue until all of our concerns and issues were discussed and resolved.* Another response of group members was: *Now that we have come together as a group where we like and respect each other, it is unreasonable for us to end our sessions.* These statements highlight a simple case of denial with several members clustering to avoid or minimize the impact of separation.

The worker, facing the above situations and probably having feelings about the separation process, will indicate to the member specifically, and the group in general, that all separations are difficult. In addition to recognizing the pain brought on by the impending end of the group, the worker should help the group to make a systematic review of the issues and concerns related to separation and model for them how the contract made during the pre-affiliation stage can be used to give members a sense of accomplishment and well being. If members are supported in their denial of separation they will miss an opportunity to learn about the various options open to them when they are forced to end personal or other relationships. Denial is a normal response to separation. If denial is not dealt with adequately, members may leave the group angry and frustrated, which could lead to personal and emotional difficulties in future social situations.

Regression

Regression is another characteristic that can surface at this stage. In such instances, regression is the inability on the part of individual members and the group to cope with the treatment tasks associated with separation. In spite of individual and group gains, members now seem unable to be close and intimate with others and often withdraw from involvement. The group may revert to an earlier stage of development by introducing and dealing with issues normally associated with the power and control or intimacy stages. This behavior is a normal part of human development and generally occurs in the face of threat or upset. The threat here, which is real, is that of losing contact with others with whom they have shared significant experiences. For example, in a group of mildly depressed patients in a hospital setting, several members echoed the same theme as separation was discussed: *I was doing very well until now. My earlier symptoms of depression have returned. I cannot reach out to any of you.* Another member noted: *As a group we are attacking each other, which has not happened since our earlier sessions. Shouldn't we continue beyond our agreed time?*

As the worker recognizes regressive behaviors among members, it is possible and indeed necessary, using the problem-solving sequence, to help the group to critically examine its treatment process. The worker may ask the group to reflect on earlier experiences when members behaved in a similar manner and what were their feelings, thoughts and behaviors at that time. As these are identified the group is encouraged to look at the similarities between earlier experiences and the present one and then be challenged in a sensitive manner to explore new ways and means of dealing with loss and separation. Hence, members are helped to recognize their regressive behaviors and the fundamental cause of these behaviors and are helped to choose other options to deal with separation.

Need to Continue

A strong need obvious during separation is for the group to continue with more sessions than has been previously agreed upon. Members may verbalize this need by saying that they have not yet achieved the treatment goals and objectives they had articulated at the beginning of the group. Or that the group has been so helpful that the group experience as it is presently constituted should continue. If this need is not dealt with sensitively, the group may attempt to threaten the worker into continuing by suggesting that their earlier dysfunctional behaviors have reoccurred. The underlying theme is that without the group, treatment gains will not be maintained.

The worker's role in such a situation is critical. To support the need to continue is likely to be in direct conflict with the organization's guidelines and policies. Not to support this need may suggest to the members a lack of understanding and caring. The worker should help members to discuss their present need in light of earlier experiences when similar feelings occurred, what each member and the group have achieved and how their achievements are in keeping with the stated goals and objectives. The relevance of this to members' everyday social functioning should be highlighted. The questions: How have you felt before when such situations arose? How did you deal with these feelings? What kinds of behavior did you act out? And do you want to function differently in the future? should be openly addressed.

Recapitulation

According to Garland et al. recapitulation may be manifested in two ways: re-enactment and review. As groups and individuals anticipate the end of their social interaction with each other, they often try to relive particular experiences from the earlier times of the relationship. For example, a group of single parents may suggest that they reenact the first group session. Such a suggestion is often accompanied by a high level of humor among members. Though given in jest such a suggestion is expected to be taken seriously.

Another aspect of recapitulation is that of reviewing in great detail various parts of the group experience from earlier sessions. Members will ask each other if they remember when ... ? This is generally followed by specific details of the event. This evidence of review and re-enactment provides an opportunity for the worker to ask the group what the specific re-enactment or review meant; what insights were gained and how these insights may be used outside of the group. The worker also asks members if there are specific things they wanted to accomplish in the group but have not done so to date. In this way members are encouraged to use the remaining sessions to maximize the accomplishment of their treatment goals and objectives.

Evaluation

A springboard for evaluation and review is provided when the group recapitulates earlier experiences in its life. As members reenact and review their experiences, the skilled worker can, in an orderly manner, ask the group members to review their treatment goals, their purposes for entering the group and how they have or have not achieved their goals. They can be asked to comment on the group treatment process as a means of achieving their individual goals.

This approach allows members to realistically review their achievements and disappointments and to receive feedback from others in the group. Recapitulation should stimulate the worker to help members complete any unfinished business they may have with each other. For instance, a member might have been critical of another throughout most of the group's life. The worker helps that member to reflect on his or her performance and the motivating factors underlying it.

A crucial aspect of evaluation is the opportunity it provides for members to learn how to constructively terminate social interaction with others. Using the agreed on contract as a focal point, all members including the worker, can systematically evaluate their achievements or lack thereof and discuss how this experience may be used in the future as members face loss. Evaluation is intimately related to the problem-solving process that should have become a part of every member's repertoire by this time. As members evaluate their performances they are often able to gain insights that help them to function more effectively. Evaluation helps all members and the worker to determine if the treatment goals have been reached and how the tasks of the group have been performed.

Summary

The process of separation is not as dramatic at the end of each session as it is when the group perceives that the end of their group experience is near. This is due to the realization that the group will be meeting again. As the end of the group approaches, members experience a sense of loss and accompanying feelings of sadness. Workers have a critical and central role to play during the separation process. The loss of a potentially valuable experience, of an opportunity to learn and to change and an opportunity to interact with others who care, must be recognized. There must be some understanding of how human beings in general and group members in particular have handled separation in the past and what options are available for handling it now and in the future.

The worker's primary thrust during this stage is to assist members to put separation in a realistic context. It is important to help the group to make connections with the separation of the group and their own endings in other social situations, whether these be voluntary or involuntary.

If the purposes for the individual, the group and the worker were not clear during the pre-affiliation stage it is unlikely that the group will end successfully. On the other hand, if the purposes, goals and objectives for all the units of this social system are clear, then the evaluative process is much more realistic and significant for all. The purposes, goals and objectives can be restated and the individual's and the group's movement toward accomplishing these purposes, goals and objectives can be reviewed.

If members have not achieved what they wanted to achieve, then reasons for the lack of achievement can be identified and discussed and commitments made to look at these processes and issues in the future. Conversely, if progress has been made toward accomplishing the purposes, goals and objectives, the individual feels a sense of satisfaction and achievement. The separation stage also provides opportunities for members to share their fears, desires, and concerns so that there is a sense of ending and not an overwhelming feeling that there is or will be unfinished business. The more ably individuals handle their terminating processes in the group and consolidate their learning, the more likely they will be able to handle similar processes outside of the treatment group. The effect of separation is a major one on the lives of human beings. If handled thoughtfully and effectively, separation provides the opportunity for maximum learning about this critical stage of human development.

QUESTIONS FOR CONSIDERATION

1. What are some of the issues that may surface for members and worker during termination?

2. How can the worker prepare to deal with issues of termination?

3. What role can the contract play during termination?

Co-Leadership

Many organizations that offer group treatment services frequently assign at least two workers to develop and take responsibility for specific groups; in some instances, workers volunteer to serve as co-leaders. Regardless of the way leaders are assigned to the group, it is seldom that a rationale for such a practice is articulated; this could lead to difficulties for the group and the workers.

Co-leadership as a method of practice is supported in most group work literature. Discovered by accident, it was found to improve and speed up the treatment process for patients in group psychotherapy (Lundin and Aronov, 1952). Over time co-leadership has become very commonplace, yet its implications and relevance to treatment has not been adequately examined (MacLennan, 1965; McGee and Schuman, 1970).

As practitioners, three questions must be addressed in order to maximize the change opportunities for clients. These questions are:

- on what basis should co-leaders be assigned?
- how can co-leadership facilitate the purpose of the group, and the achievement of the treatment goals and objectives?
- what are the major issues and concerns for the workers and the clients, both individually and collectively?

The Organization's Responsibility for Co-Leadership

The organization in which group treatment is practiced must take responsibility for the assignment of leaders to the treatment group. In assigning leaders, the primary purpose for which the group is set up must be given careful and serious consideration. Will two workers be more effective than a single worker in guiding the group toward achieving its treatment goals? The assignment of a co-leader should be for the benefit of the clients rather than to meet the needs of the worker.

In pre-screening workers for co-leadership, the organization must ensure that those assigned demonstrate some competence in the majority of the following areas as have been identified by Brandler and Roman, (1981, p. 195) namely:

- modeling expression of feelings;

- problem solving;
- the ability to present different perspectives;
- modeling healthy conflict resolution;
- the ability to provide the group with a range of transferential material;
- mutual respect for the opposite sex;
- an ability to share power and accept an equal distribution of same;
- an ability to effectively manage explosive situations while recognizing individual needs;
- an ability to carry on and provide continuity in the event of the co-leader's absence or other crisis situation within the organization; and
- an ability to be supportive in emotionally charged situations.

There may be other reasons for assigning two leaders, such as offering training to less experienced workers and students, to provide some checks and balances on workers and to challenge and stimulate each other.

For example, in a group for separated and divorced parents whose members do not respect or trust persons of the other sex, two workers of opposite sex can model mutual respect for each other and in a real way demonstrate an equal sharing of power between them. Moreover, co-workers are in a unique position to display how conflicts between them can be resolved in a healthy and constructive manner. There will be differences of interpretation around the problems that members bring to the group. It would be very helpful for members to see both workers talking about their understanding of the problems identified by members in order to see if there are disagreements of interpretation, and then explore an interpretation and approach that would benefit clients. In this manner, workers can demonstrate for the clients how areas of conflict or difficulty can be resolved through discussion and negotiation.

Not only is it important to be guided by the purpose for which the group will be established, but also by the following:

- the goals of the sponsoring organization;
- the competence and level of skill of each worker; and
- the compatibility between workers vis-à-vis the group treatment task.

If the organization is committed to achieving such dual goals as enhancing the social functioning of clients and maximizing student learning, the agency representative responsible for service must decide which goal takes priority. Ideally, the question that must be answered unequivocally is: how can clients be best served to meet their enhancement goals and at the same time provide a good learning experience for students?

A co-leadership assignment must recognize the individual competencies and level of skill of each worker. Every effort should be made to assign workers who have compatible levels of skill and competence in group treatment. To assign workers of dissimilar or unequal levels of skill or competence is to risk the domination of one worker by the other or the heightening of feelings of inadequacy and incompetence in the less competent worker. Neophytes and students are often placed in such a position. Admittedly it may provide a forum for learning, but such a practice should not be entered into with out adequate discussion and involvement of the workers to be assigned.

The compatibility of the workers assigned to co-leadership is essential in order to achieve treatment goals. A thorough assessment of the respective workers' philosophies about helping clients, whether in an individual, family or group context must be made. Persons of conflicting philosophies are very likely to take their differences into the group to the disadvantage of the clients. The same is true for the theoretical orientations that are held by the workers. There is no suggestion that these differences are always a hindrance to treatment; however, if they are not addressed openly by the workers, there is the potential for treatment to be sabotaged by conflicting ideologies.

Worker Preparation for Co-Leadership

Just as organizations are expected to prepare for co-leadership so are the workers who are assigned to a co-leadership team. This preparation should revolve around the following:

- individual competencies, skills, preferences and experience as these relate to group treatment;
- theoretical orientation and personal philosophies regarding group treatment and problem solving;
- roles and responsibilities to be assumed by each worker;
- time commitment for planning, monitoring and evaluating the group treatment process; and
- establishing dynamic working procedures for conflict resolution.

After the workers have been selected for the task there must be discussion between themselves about their individual skills, competencies, preferences and experience as these relate to group treatment. For example, workers should honestly discuss their strengths and weaknesses as group workers, the relevance of their training and their preferences regarding approaches to group treatment. Relevant group related practice experiences should also be discussed. Such discussion should indicate to both workers whether they are capable of functioning as equal partners or not. Even though their backgrounds may suggest that they are at different levels of competence and skill, they should be able to decide how each could complement the other in the group treatment process.

If, for example, one worker is committed to a psycho-dynamic theoretical model of practice, while the other prefers a Gestalt orientation, it is possible that there may be contrary directions pursued by the co-leaders. One worker may be trying to get the group as a whole to gain insight and understanding in a cooperative and facilitative way. The other worker is likely to have a group member to be the focus and at the same time be encouraging other members to pursue a similar approach, hoping that the member who has been singled out will gain some understanding and insight of his or her feelings, thoughts and behaviors in the here and now. Clearly the respective workers' philosophy of group treatment and use of the problem-solving method as a way of facilitating the treatment process must be clarified. This clarity helps workers to determine appropriate interventions at the various stages of group development.

The co-leaders must also decide on the duties, roles and responsibilities each of them is to have in and out of the group sessions. For example, which worker will be responsible for the physical arrangements related to the group's functioning? Which one will be responsible for recording? Will one of them assume responsibility for being more assertive and confrontative in the group; or will both play nurturing and supportive roles? Will the roles assumed by each leader be complementary or in direct opposition?

Working together as co-leaders will not necessarily be more time efficient than working alone. Both workers must be prepared to allot time for regular planning, monitoring and evaluating of the group treatment process. Before each session, time should be spent anticipating what is likely to happen in the group and what each worker is prepared to do given their projections on outcomes in the group. Similarly, time should be spent after the group sessions reflecting on the treatment process and their individual roles and responsibilities. There must also be an evaluation of how worker, clients and organization are individually and collectively moving toward the achievement of their established goals.

It is necessary to establish dynamic working procedures for the resolution of conflict in the group whether that conflict arises between members, between members and leaders, or between the leaders themselves. If, as is likely, there is a disagreement during a given session, the workers should have decided before the session how such disagreements will be handled.

Benefits of Co-Leadership

The literature indicates that there are several benefits to be achieved through a co-leadership. Among these benefits are:

- sharing responsibility for the group treatment process;
- receiving and giving emotional support to each other;
- the opportunity for objectivity during complex dynamic interactions;
- assisting each other in setting and enforcing limits;
- modeling different styles of interaction; and
- structuring leader roles to meet the needs of the group.

One of the benefits of co-leadership, particularly to the neophyte, is that of sharing the responsibility for the group treatment process (Levine, 1980). As noted earlier, there are certain administrative and mechanical tasks that need to be done for each group. Being able to share these tasks makes it easier for both leaders and probably provokes less anxiety. It seems reasonable to assume that if anxiety is decreased worker effectiveness will improve and this will ultimately benefit the whole group.

Co-leadership provides for the receiving and giving of emotional support between co-leaders (Galinsky and Schopler, 1980). As workers function together they come to see each other as allies trying to achieve the same goals. If successful, this allows each worker to maximize and fully use his or her unique leadership skills and abilities and this will in turn enhance group treatment. Objectivity is crucial when one leader is involved in complex, dynamic interactions with one or several group members. For example, a group leader may be scapegoated by several members without having any awareness of how he or she might have provoked the scapegoating. One worker may help the other worker and the group to understand what has occurred.

Co-leadership may enhance the worker's ability to establish and enforce limits. This is not to suggest that co-workers should overemphasize a policing role in the group. Such a role may be symptomatic of what is occurring in the group and must therefore be dealt with in the context of the group (Shulman, 1988). Helping each other to set and enforce limits is likely to model for members how they too may be able to set and enforce limits among themselves and even outside of the group.

A benefit directly related to the group treatment process involves the ability of two group leaders to model different styles of interaction. For example, co-leaders may model more effective communication methods or may provide the opportunity for group members to observe productive conflict resolution techniques (Yalom, 1975).

Of critical importance is the structuring of the co-leaders' roles to meet the needs of the group. For example, a client who is a substance abuser may best be helped if one leader plays a confrontational role while the other plays a more supportive role to demonstrate alternative ways of interacting with individuals. Such a scenario provides for confrontation, while at the same time ensuring emotional support for individual group members. Such functioning frees members to work in an atmosphere that may be uncomfortable but safe.

Disadvantages of Co-Leadership

Not all of the effects of co-leadership are as positive as the ones discussed above. With the assistance of Galinsky and Schopler (1980), and Yalom (1975), the following list of disadvantages is identified:

- co-leadership is expensive;
- the reciprocal reduction of effectiveness of co-leaders–effectiveness of the individual leader is reduced; and
- negative relationships between co-leaders.

Galinsky and Schopler (1980), and Yalom (1975), posit that one of the primary administrative arguments against co-leadership is a monetary one. Obviously having two leaders conduct a group is substantially more expensive than having one leader. Not only is the practice a drain on the financial resources of an organization, it requires considerably more time as leaders are expected to meet repeatedly to co-ordinate their efforts and discuss their strategies and interventions (Yalom, 1975). Hence, the effectiveness of the co-leadership service must be carefully weighed against its added expense of time and money.

One worker may well reduce the effectiveness of the other. Each worker may avoid experiencing the full weight of responsibility for the group and its members (Levine, 1980, p. 35). It is easy to see how one worker may expect the other to perform particular tasks and duties while the other worker makes the same assumption. Unquestionably, this detracts from the overall effectiveness of the team, which in turn detracts from the effectiveness of the group.

It is possible that the relationship between the co-leaders may not be helpful to the group treatment process. According to a number of authors, the relationship between the co-leaders is crucial to treatment (MacLennan, 1965; Rabin, 1967; Galinsky and Schopler, 1980). Ideally, the leaders should have the same theoretical perspective and leadership styles and be able to communicate well, without harboring thoughts or feelings that would negatively affect each other. Realistically, however, co-leaders do not often complement each other and neither do they always agree. Hence, conflicts, competition and power struggles may be imposed on a group to the detriment of the members and the treatment process.

One effect of this incompatibility may be for group members to attempt and succeed at splitting the workers. Clients have an investment in splitting the workers if it will protect them from having to deal with their own difficulties. Further, a dysfunctional relationship between the workers may promote perceptions and misconceptions in the group about power and authority and create such an imbalance that clients will be unable to achieve their goals. Not only will clients be unable to pursue their goals in the group, members will be hindered from developing healthy ways of communicating outside of the group, which could have been their ultimate purpose for entering the group. Modeling incompatibility in the group could be potentially devastating for vulnerable clients.

In summary, there are pros and cons for the use of co-leadership in group treatment. So too are there pros and cons for individual or single leadership. The worker needs to be well grounded in the same theories and knowledge as would be two or more leaders. Individual leadership for many practitioners would remain their preference.

QUESTIONS FOR CONSIDERATION

1. On what basis would you decide to use a co-leadership structure in group treatment?

2. What worker preparation is necessary before effective co-leadership is undertaken?

3. How would you attempt to evaluate the effectiveness of co-leadership in group treatment?

4. Are there ways of using the disadvantages of co-leadership to the benefit of group members?

SECTION 2: SUGGESTED READINGS

- Alissi, A.A. (Ed.). (1980). *Perspectives on Social Group Work Practice*. New York: The Free Press.
- Bennis, W.G., Benne, K.D., Chin R., and Corey K.E. (Eds.). (1976). *The Planning of Change (3rd ed.)*. New York: Holt, Rinehart and Winston.
- Bernstein, S. (Ed.). (1965). *Explorations in Social Group Work*. Boston: Boston University School of Social Work.
- Bradford, L.P. (Ed.). (1978). *Group Development (2nd ed)*. La Jolla, California: University Associates.
- Brandler, S. and Roman, C.P. (1981). *Group Work: Skills and Strategies for Effective Interventions*. New York. Haworth Press.
- Budman, S.H., Bennet, M.J., and Wisneski, M.J. (1980). Short-term group psychotherapy: An adult developmental model. *International Journal of Group Psychotherapy, 30*, 63–75.
- Carbino, R. (1982). Group work with natural parents in permanency planning. *Social Work with Groups, 5(4)*, 7–30.
- Corey, G., and Corey, M.S. (1982). *Groups: Process and Practice (2nd ed.)*. Monterey, California: Brooks/Cole Publishing Co.
- Corey, G., Corey, M.S., Callanan, P.J., and Russell, J.M. (1982). *Group Techniques*. Monterey, California: Brooks/Cole Publishing Co.
- Currie, David W. (1983). A Toronto model. *Social-work-with-Groups:* 6(3–4) 179–188.
- Davis, F.B. and Lohr, N.E. (1971). Special problems with the use of cotherapists in group psychotherapy. *International Journal of Group Psychotherapy,* 21, 143–158.
- Dimock, H. (1976). *Planning Group Development*. Montreal: Concordia University.
- Epstein, N. (1976). Techniques of brief therapy with children and parents. *Social Casework, 57*, 317–323.
- Galinsky, M.J., and Schopler, J.H. (1980). Structuring co-leadership in social work training. *Social Work with Groups,* 3(4), 51–63.
- Garvin, C.D. (1981). *Contemporary Group Work*. New Jersey: Prentice-Hall, Inc.
- Getzel, G. (1982). Group work with kin and friends caring for the elderly. *Social Work with Groups, 5(4)*, 91–102.
- Gitterman, A., and Shulman, L. (Eds.)(1986). *Mutual Aid Groups and the Life Cycle*. Itasca, Illinois: F.E. Peacock Publishers.
- Glassman, U., and Kates, L. (1983). Authority themes and worker-group transactions: Additional dimensions to the stages of group development. *Social Work with Groups, 6(2)*, 33–52.
- Glassman, U., and Kates, L. (1990). *Group Work. A Humanistic Approach*. Newburg Park, California: Sage Publications.
- Gordy, P. (1983). Group work that supports adult victims of childhood incest. *Social Casework, 64*, 300–307.
- Holman, S.L. (1985). A group program for borderline mothers and their toddlers. *International Journal of Group Psychotherapy, 35*, 79–93.
- Hurley, D.J. (1974). Resistance and work in adolescent groups. *Social Work With Groups, 7(4)*, 71–81.
- Korda, Lois J. and Pancrazio, James J. (1989). Limiting negative outcome in group practice. *Journal for Specialists in Group Work:* 14(2), 112–120.
- Lee, J.A., and Park, D.N. (1978). A group approach to the depressed adolescent girl in foster care. *American Journal of Orthopsychiatry, 48(3)*, 516–527.
- Levine, B. (1980). Co-leadership approaches to learning group work. *Social Work with Groups,* 3(4), 35–38.

- Lewis, Karen G. (1989). Teaching gender issues to male/female group therapists. Special Issue: Variations on teaching and supervising group therapy. *Journal of Independent Social Work:* 3(4), 125–139.

- Lowy, L. (1982). Social group work with vulnerable older persons: A theoretical perspective. *Social Work With Groups, 5(2),* 21–32.

- Lundin, W. and Aronov, B. (1952). The use of co-therapists in group psychotherapy, *Journal of Consulting Psychology,* (vol 16, pp. 76–80).

- MacLennan, B.W. (1965). Co-therapy. *International Journal of Group Psychotherapy,* 15, 154–165.

- Nobler, H. (1980). A peer group for therapists: Successful experience in sharing. *International Journal of Group Psychotherapy, 30(1),* 51–62.

- Ormont, L.R. (1984). The leader's role in dealing with aggression in groups. *International Journal of Group Psychotherapy, 34,* 553–572.

- Pfeifer, G.D., and Weinstock-Savoy, D. (1984). Peer culture and the organization of self and object representations in children's psychotherapy groups. *Social Work With Groups, 7(4),* 39–56.

- Scharlach, A.E. (1985). Social group work with institutionalized elders: A task centered approach. *Social Work With Groups, 8(3).*

- Shulman, L. (1968). *A casebook of social work with groups: The mediating model.* New York: Council on Social Work Education.

- Shulman, L. (1988). *Dynamics and skills for group work: An interactional approach.* Workshop conducted: Waterloo, Canada.

- Smith, J.D., Walsh, R.J., and Richardson, M.A. (1985). The clown club: A structured fantasy approach to group therapy with the latency-age child. *International Journal of Group Psychotherapy, 35,* 49–64.

- Starak, Y. (1981). Co-leadership: A new look at sharing group work. *Social Work with Groups,* 4(¾), 145–157.

- Winter, S.K. (1976). Developmental stages in the roles and concerns of group co-leaders. *Small Group Behavior,* 7, 349–362.

- Yalom, Irvin, (1985). *The Theory and Practice of Group Psychotherapy,* (3rd. ed.) New York: Basic Books, Inc.

CASE STUDIES IN GROUP TREATMENT

The following case studies offer the practitioner opportunities to examine and explore some of the many auspices under which group treatment is practiced, the range of practice options possible in any given situation and how theory informs practice in group treatment. It is hoped that discussion of these case studies, which have been provided by several practitioners, will be encouraged by persons wanting to develop skill in this area of study.

A major task for the practitioner is to understand each client in his or her unique and diverse context. This understanding will direct the activities of the practitioner towards helping the client to establish clear goals, and to be able to use the group treatment process to help the client to realize these goals. The group treatment process, regardless of the specific client, is similar and has as its primary objective helping the client to achieve their treatment goals.

.

SECTION 3: CONTENTS

A Treatment Group for Male Survivors of Sexual Abuse

Robert Basso

ociety has been slow to respond to the issue of male sexual abuse, and in the past has even denied that men can be victims of traumatic sexual abuse. Given the needs of these men, it is essential that practitioners be more active in providing group treatment services to deal with the results of the abuse. Human service agencies need to be aware of the issues of this specific population as they relate to group treatment and to devise programs that make it easier for these survivors to seek services (Briere, Evans, Runtz and Wall, 1988; Bruckner and Johnson, 1987; Sebold, 1987).

An agency's awareness of the need for a group for male survivors grew after wives and partners of the men had requested help for them. This agency had been providing group work services to women who had been abused for more than a decade. The provision of group work services for male survivors of abuse was a new practice direction for the agency and was a new service in the community.

The author co-led a group for male survivors of child sexual abuse in a community counseling setting. The group was designed to permit group participants an opportunity to discover, develop and explore the issue of being male and having lived through the trauma of being sexually abused as a child. Male survivors "frequently suffer silently, victimizing themselves. The male victims feel ashamed, fear that they are mentally ill, and fear disbelief by parents and other adults" (Vander Mey, 1988, p.61).

Group Leadership

Preparation for leadership with this group included extensive reading on clinical issues related to men who had been sexually abused in childhood. Professional readiness included the creation of the statement of purposes and treatment goals, the development of group selection criteria, and the design and layout of group activities. The group format and processes were conceptualized according to the Boston Model of group practice.

Group Purposes

This group was designed to accomplish many purposes. The first was to provide an opportunity for participants to verbalize, share and explore the issue of childhood sexual abuse and the resulting trauma with other survivors. The second was to assist men in developing a variety of coping strategies. Survivors of childhood sexual abuse struggle with socio-emotional issues related to family, co-workers and friends. The third was the agency's purpose to provide services to an underserved population, therefore meeting an agency mandate to furnish assistance to those whose needs had not been addressed in the community.

Group Treatment Goals

Group treatment goals were aimed at reducing feelings of being alone with this problem, increasing feelings of adequacy in the members' current life situation and providing an opportunity to appraise their life experiences within the group's supportive environment.

Feelings of isolation are common among male survivors. Group provides a means to alleviate the feelings of detachment by realizing that their experiences are not unique. Men can identify with others who have gone through similar life situations.

Sexual abuse can corrode and tarnish one's self-esteem. The residual feelings can be dealt with in a group through discussions of those past events. The development of new insights and understandings can result in a changed perception of oneself as a competent, caring being.

Group provides members with the opportunity to re-evaluate their life's experiences in a supportive environment. This environment provides the key condition for work to occur. It offers members the prospect of completing the first steps in each member's life journey to repair his hurts and emotional wounds (Brucker and Johnson, 1987). In addition, group members are assisted in developing specific goals in relation to their feelings of self-worth, their behaviors in relation to themselves and others and, with the support of the group, attempt to achieve their individual goals.

Selection

Leadership preparation activities concluded with the pre-screening interviews with potential members. These interviews served to ensure a goodness of fit for the group's purposes and the potential member's needs for help. We asked: Is there a chance this group can assist the member, and how? Also, we assessed each man's readiness to give and receive feedback, and his overall level of trust. A man's willingness to identify abuse was a central key in assessing future participation in the group. Could the men see the impacts on their lives, that is, on family, intimacy and peer relationships?

Treatment Issues

The problems that the male survivors identified and brought to the group included an inability to trust others, feelings of low self-esteem and guilt, and experiences of poor social skills. We anticipated that when using the Boston Model, we would encounter treatment concerns at the various stages of group development for this population of men. The pre-affiliation stage may be prolonged because of the special attention to the men's trust needs. Low self-esteem, feelings of guilt and poor social skills complicate the group's movement through this stage and the following stages of power and control and intimacy. The surviving males came in for assistance because of related social, marital and family problems, not necessarily for help directly related to their histories of abuse.

Co-Leadership

Both leaders were committed to the processes and directions at the out-set. Any confusion about the goals or disrespect shown towards the other leader would translate into chaos in the group's processes. They were able to challenge each other and model this in group for the members to experience.

The leader's roles can be complimentary in nature, that is, process observer, discussion leader. The leader's varied life experiences and diversity help to stimulate identification and transference issues. Both agreed to debrief and review the group's progress after each meeting.

Evaluation

Evaluation was an ongoing process beginning at the start of the group. At the midpoint, leaders assisted members in reviewing their progress towards their stated goals. Are the goals the ones that they need to work on? Do changes need to be made regarding the chosen goals?

Each member assessed his progress towards the goals that he chose at the beginning of the group. The leaders asked the members to rate their progress towards the completion of each personal goal on a scale of one to five, enquired what else needed to be done in order to move closer towards the achievement of the specific goal, and made note of the steps needed to reach goal attainment.

The group as a whole commented on the vitality and helpfulness of the group in assisting the members to reach their goals. This was an opportunity to assess the group atmosphere-of-helpfulness. As the group was perceived as helpful, it was able to assist members to identify and capitalize on the helpful processes. If the group had not been helpful, discussion about what needed to change or happen differently in order to take the group to new directions in the group would have taken place.

Group leaders also had insights into the group's achievement of, or ability to work towards, the treatment goals. The leader's comments stimulated further discussion about the work that the group was undertaking or that needed to be examined. The leaders' reviews and commentary about the group's functioning supported the work and conditions needed to achieve the stated goals.

Goal Orientation

Having a goal orientation in group work provides direction and allows adaption as needed. It respects the process of change as members identify and modify their own change goals over time. It assists members to see and have a sense of their own history of change, the steps they employed and the processes they used. This sense of a member's unique personal journey can be the basis of information that can be used in the future when he encounters new challenges or similar problems.

Conclusion

Society has been slow to respond to men's abuse issues, even denied that men can be victims of traumatic sexual abuse. Given the needs of these men, it is essential that we be more active in providing group treatment services to deal with the results of the abuse. Human services agencies need to be aware of the issues of this specific population as they relate to group treatment, and to devise programs to make it easier for these survivors to seek services.

Substance and Alcohol Abuse

Edcil Wickham

There has been an increased awareness in society regarding the prevalence and impact of substance abuse in populations as early as pre-teen up to and including the elderly. It is suggested that the root causes of the problem may be in the extent to which children have or feel some attachment to parental figures in their lives. It is also proposed that substance abuse could be understood through social learning theory and/or genetic predisposition. Regardless of the manifestation of the problem, group treatment offers the opportunity for clients who have abused alcohol and/or drugs to attach to the group and its members in a way that would promote sobriety and reduce the risk of relapse. It should be noted that most of the clients coming for substance or alcohol abuse treatment are there involuntarily.

By involuntary, it is meant that most clients seeking treatment have been in some way influenced to attend some sort of treatment for their difficulties with substances or alcohol. This is likely to manifest itself when the group comes together for the first time in the members' ambivalence in acknowledging that they have a problem with substance or alcohol and in their admission that it was an employer or partner or physician or the justice system that influenced their coming forward for treatment. This involuntary status can be expected to make it difficult for members to acknowledge personal responsibility for their problems and also deny that their difficulties are as serious as has been suggested by others.

Group Leadership Preparation

One practitioner was assigned the task of facilitating a group of approximately eight people who had varying levels of difficulty reducing their dependence on alcohol and/or drugs. Potential members for this group were all seeking treatment involuntarily.

During the pre-screening, clients were encouraged to think about goals they would like to achieve and to be prepared to write these down and discuss them during the first group including how they would know that they had achieved these goals. In doing so, the context for the clients' work was clearly established as theirs, with the leader providing guidance and strategies towards achieving the clients' goals. It was expected that there would be some difficulty formulating goals since most of the clients were not there voluntarily. The leader must be prepared to address the involuntary status of group members in order to assist them towards goal setting and achievement.

Stages—From Beginning to Separation

During the first session, the clients were asked to introduce themselves in a manner that allowed them to show their goals and those indicators that would attest to success at goal attainment throughout the group. One of the group goals was to have members indicate how they would help each other to achieve their goals. In this way, the worker collected information on (1) what would be discussed and, (2) how it would be discussed throughout the group. A culmination of this stage was reached when there was a clear understanding of the topics to be discussed and how these would be discussed. Without this understanding of context and process, the group would not likely have moved to the next stage of development, mainly power and control.

In the next stage of group development, matters of power and control were foremost in the minds and activities of the group. The issues that surfaced each week demonstrated that the clients had become attached to the group and its members. These stages parallel those that children go through as they become attached to their parents and/or significant adults in their lives. Some of the themes that emerged were relevance of group, the ability of the leader to be helpful, the ability of the members' to relate to others in an unhealthy manner and the scapegoating of members. These themes need to be addressed carefully and with sensitivity since they relate to issues of authority and who has the authority to say and do what. As these issues were resolved for the mutual benefit and satisfaction of group members, the themes related to intimacy came to the fore, for example, how members function in matters related to their families and their employers.

As the group moves through various stages, it should be evident that members are forming significant attachments to each other and may well be using these attachments to gain support in their struggles for sobriety. It is possible that members may decide to use each other to assist them in achieving their goals of sobriety and reduce risks of relapse. In fact, in this particular group, members chose to attend other meetings together such as Alcoholics Anonymous and also to phone each other in times of stress. Throughout the group, the risk of personal losses was constantly discussed.

Therefore as the group comes to separation, members openly discuss gains made and how these were made, and the extent to which these gains can be reinforced for the future.

Most members were able to talk about the improved sense of self and how they were changing in relation to work, family and friends. This evaluation, even though personal, is a significant measure of how clients are able to achieve their goals. The achievement of goals will reinforce for members the need to set clearly articulated goals for changing affect, cognition or behavior and how these gains can be enhanced outside of the group. Through the support of each member the risks of relapse is minimized. These gains can be maintained through the use of each other when there is no group to attend.

Group Treatment: Administrators Dealing with Stress

Catherine Martin

The request for a social worker to provide group intervention for the "leadership" within a small rural community hospital came from the vice-president of the hospital. It was decided to respond to the leaders and/or managers' need for support through a transition from working within small independent hospitals to amalgamating the administrations of two hospitals. The vice-president had the authority to authorize this expenditure for leaders and managers. Throughout, the group process funding was assured.

The Group

The group consisted of five motivated, dedicated, intelligent, responsible leaders: Dorothy, Joanne, Betty, Maureen and Kim. They needed support to adapt to complex change within their work environment. Changing roles, responsibilities and collaborating with new colleagues within a destabilized health care climate were the expectations. To support, encourage and achieve this shift change was the intervention requested of the practitioner.

Context

The context is reflective of the changing socio-economic and political climate of the community. Both levels of government had reduced funding to a number of public sectors including health care as a cost-cutting measure to enable tax cuts and balance budgets. As a result of the governments' policies, hospitals were encouraged to amalgamate and to share responsibilities for a number of areas, such as patient programs, nutrition services, physical plant and education.

Setting

The setting for holding group sessions was established at the one hospital where it was easiest for all members to meet and where there was a room where all could gather, assured they could talk without interruption and where the sense of privacy and keeping confidences felt secured.

Preparation

Preparation for the group began with the social worker consulting with the group members to secure a commitment to attend the first session. Of the group of seven, all were women except for one gentleman. At the outset he declared he was not comfortable with a "support" group; he self-selected exclusion. Additionally, one woman, Annie, was ambivalent about joining. The five who elected to attend the group clarified the contract with the social worker over the first two sessions.

Purpose

The purpose of the group was to obtain support for the individual leaders to cope with their changing roles within a changing system and to provide support to one another. The goals set to achieve this end included increasing awareness of issues of power and control, setting boundaries, putting self-care action plans in place, and learning to accept more empathy for the self and demonstrate more compassion for others in the process. Expression of affect, respectful discussion of thoughts and opinions, exploration of new behaviors in the group within the context of a safe and trusting climate were addressed as part of the contract. In short, this was a learning lab for mutual aid and personal and professional development. The group agreed to meet on a monthly basis with the social worker over the next seven months. This particular social worker was chosen because of a combination of her group work experience and her knowledge of health care as well as the dynamics of a rural community. Evaluation of the group's goals would be part of an ongoing process.

Treatment Issues

Issues within the pre-affiliation and affiliation stage witnessed the members spending time trying to find ways to include their co-worker who was ambivalent about attending. Each member had approached her, explaining the benefits of giving and receiving support in the context of the group. They expressed their frustration that she refused their invitation to join yet remained negative and unhappy with her work. The social worker's questioning whether their efforts paralleled their own sense of ambivalence led to their clarification that they really did want to attend to the goals they had set and to come to terms with her refusal to join.

This moved the group more surely into learning how to deal with rejection, lack of acceptance and clarity around how much responsibility was theirs to support their peer and how much responsibility belonged to her. A broad range of feelings, such as anger, guilt, helplessness and sadness, were expressed and acknowledged. They accepted the reality of their colleague's decision to do things differently. Their goals of self- and/or other support and empathy were met, and they experimented with new behaviors by setting new limits for themselves around responsibility.

During the intimacy and differentiation stages of treatment, they helped one another through some challenging, difficult periods. Maureen was confronted with the reality of the hierarchy of power within the health care system: that physicians, government officials and the boards of governors held more power than other stakeholders. The lack of respect some members of these groups demonstrated towards them was a source of distress. To maintain self-esteem within this system, all the group members were called upon to maintain respect for one another in their communications in spite of what they witnessed and to sustain their support for each other. Contained by the growing sense of safety and trust within the group, the worker encouraged the members to risk more by revealing their authentic selves. When Dorothy wept openly about her fears of meeting so many new demands in two hospitals, all members listened and all lent support. Two colleagues challenged her self-image as the "super leader." This ultimately led Dorothy to experiment with saying no to some tasks, prioritizing others and promising to revise her self-care action plan, that is, to go home at least once each week at 5 p.m.

During this stage, the group was also accepting of Kim's input as the newest, youngest member of the leaders' group. As she had recently been hired from outside their rural system, she was able to offer objective, fresh points of view, which the others considered respectfully.

When Betty became seriously ill, her group members rallied to give her comfort and encouragement. When she announced a few sessions later, after her recovery and return to work, that she had decided to retire, they began a mourning process. The others expressed their sadness to see her leave their midst, but also they expressed their happiness that she showed she was taking charge of her own well-being. The social worker wondered if Betty's announcement could be foreshadowing the ending of their group or at least the upcoming change in their group constellation and possibly another change in the hospital system. There was information circulating that perhaps the amalgamation of the hospitals would not work, that a return to individual governance would occur. This possibility prompted feelings of disbelief and disappointment. This group of leaders had put their hearts and souls into adapting to the change and now they feared, as Dorothy stated: "All of our good work will go to waste." With encouragement from the worker, they explored their values around the kind of efforts they had made and what they would continue to do if faced with a reversal to the old ways. With Joanne, the informal leader of the group initiating the process, they began to explore together the "all in the same boat" phenomenon. The group worked through the issue to the point where they proclaimed they would continue to do their work with honesty, respect and diligence and that they would be true to their own personal integrity and loyal to the mission of the organization. In keeping with their goals, they would set boundaries for themselves around what they were able to offer as leaders. Throughout this stage of treatment, they showed one another immense respect for their differences. It would be all right if Maureen sought a position elsewhere if she judged that her ethics were compromised.

Evaluation

Evaluation of the group was continuous as planned in the contract. When a snowstorm prevented the social worker from reaching the hospital for a session, she was greeted at the rescheduled session with their upset that she had decided not to press on. After all, they had made it to the session. Upon receiving the worker's apology and attending further to the process, we learned that the group really wished she had been there because they needed her help regarding their colleague who had refused the group originally and who was having great difficulties dealing with the next round of change. They acknowledged that they wanted their group to continue as it provided a sense of structure, constancy and trust in a changing, insecure environment.

Conclusion

These leaders within a particular hospital administration are described by the social worker as real, open, authentic, caring and responsible individuals. For the social worker it was an honor to facilitate achievement of their goals, witness their growth in self, growth in their strength and determination and their compassion for others.

Men Who Abuse: A Treatment Group for First Nations Men

Steven Thibodeau and William Pelech

irst Nations[1] females are twice as likely to suffer from female partner abuse than are other Canadian women (Moyer, 1992, p. 393). This phenomenon has caused government agencies and First Nations communities to allocate resources to address this concern. First Nations communities in Southern Alberta, and in the Blackfoot Confederacy in particular, have been instrumental in establishing treatment groups for men who batter their wives. Their primary goal is to reduce the level of violence against women by reintroducing First Nations men to traditional values, beliefs and behaviors that espouse greater respect and harmony in their martial relationships. There is an awakening of traditional attitudes that foster greater harmony and respect between men and women. These attitudes also press for greater accountability and confrontation of abusive behavior. Community members are beginning to be challenged on their abusive attitudes and inaction towards family violence.

The reserves are fairly impermeable to non-tribal members, resulting in entry to few newcomers. Also, a tight kinship may have a deleterious effect on the dynamics of family violence initiatives for male batterers. When family violence initiatives are held in a participant's home community, it is inevitable that the group will most likely include the participant's father, uncle, brother, nephew, brothers-in-law or other close family members. These men deeply value family loyalty regardless of how misguided or misplaced that loyalty may be. This becomes a particularly poignant clinical issue, as the backbone of most family violence initiatives is based on the principles of confrontation and accountability. The presence of strong family loyalties may thwart the group facilitator's efforts to promote such principles.

Preparation

Planning for the delivery of an effective treatment groups is particularly important in an Aboriginal community. Indeed, in the case of a new family violence treatment group, the writers would devote as long as six months to the development phase. The group worker needs to understand the political structure of the community as well as the network of extended families and their interrelationships. Such knowledge enables the worker to anticipate potential concerns of the community members. It also enables the worker to more effectively implement the most important aspect of planning in Aboriginal communities: consultation with key informants and stakeholders. Time must be made available for the group worker to visit with Elders and influential family members.

First Nations treatment groups must contend with many of the practical issues faced by most mainstream models. Confidentiality is a sensitive issue. Participants are advised that standardized records are kept on each group session but they are stored securely and only the facilitator has access to them, unless directed otherwise by the participant. Legal ramifications and responsibility of issues pertaining to confidentiality are also discussed. Fortunately funding is not a concern for this group, as First Nations administrators provide it. Further transportation could also be provided if required.

Group Purpose

The purpose of the group was for men to understand themselves better and to learn different ways of acting in their relationships. In this group men learned from each other, Elders, and the group workers. Topics normally discussed included improving communication skills, strengthening relationships, anger management, assertiveness skills, coping skills, attitudes, values, beliefs and spirituality in relationships, holistic living and social constraints. The therapeutic climate included spiritual tools: prayers, purification ceremonies (such as smudging) and feasts. Elders often took a lead role in facilitating these traditional rituals. These activities not only helped to establish a conductive climate, they also served to empower those who possessed traditional knowledge, and might have increased the receptivity of group members to culturally rooted options and strategies to violent behavior (Hart, 1996; Morrisette, McKensie and Morrissette, 1999).

Group Treatment Goals

There are several fundamental goals for these groups, which include:
- Understanding the safety needs of the abused women;
- Accepting responsibility for their violent behavior;

- Stopping the use of violence to maintain power and control in the relationship;

- Influencing the men's behavior so that they do not re-offend;

- Understanding that partner abuse is perpetrated by women's political, social and economic inequality and is supported by culturally based sexism (Dobash and Dobash, 1992; Myers, 1996).

Selection of Clients

A potential participant had to state his readiness and willingness to participate in the group, a willingness to refrain from alcohol or drug use for two days prior to the day of the group, and be able to identify some degree of conflict in his relationship with his significant other. The pre-screening offered the opportunity to determine if the man was ready for the treatment, to develop an assessment of the participant's strengths and areas of concern and to understand the purpose for his involvement in the group. Issues discussed at the pre-screening phase included identifying the participant's expectation of the group, his specific goals and the group's expectation of him.

Efforts were made to encourage fathers to participate with their sons to promote exploration of intergenerational issues. Older and veteran members (those who had attended several cycles of the group) served as mentors and role models for younger or newer members. Veteran members were described as forming the four foundational poles of the group tepee, while the contributions of new members were portrayed as adding new poles to strengthen the structure. In this way each member's contributions and their peer support were viewed as a form of service to the group and a way of making amends for their abusive behavior.

Treatment Issues

The group convened one evening a week and lasted from two to two and one-half hours. The setting was made as comfortable as possible by providing soft chairs and quiet and private surroundings. Native artefacts and artwork by local workers were tastefully displayed. As these were open group sessions, participants could enter the group at any time, which made it difficult to control the number of participants. However, the average number was about five men, which appeared to be an ideal number.

Normally each weekly session began with a check-in round, where men shared their experiences between sessions. In keeping with traditional Aboriginal norms for group behavior, the check-in proceeded in a clockwise fashion. The check-in also provided an opportunity for new members to introduce themselves. In a similar fashion, each session ended with a check-in round, where members were asked to share what they had found most helpful about the session. The closing check-in was particularly important in reducing agitation or arousal associated with interactions during the session. Past experience has shown that members who leave a group session in a state of heightened arousal are at high risk to re-offend.

Stages of Group Development

All of the members of the First Nations group are known to each other in some way. The session began with the Elder taking on a unique role in the group as spiritual and/or cultural leader, while the male and female facilitators welcomed each member to the group. The Elder opened the group with prayer and a smudge, and at the same time explained the importance of the ceremonies. Small talk revolved around the various relationships that existed between members of the group and led to a discussion of each members goals, and how these goals might be achieved through the use of the groups processes.

Alliances appeared to be forming between several of the members around the matter of the negative, manipulative role of women that had created difficulties for each of the men, as they saw it. The female co-leader reminded members of a group rule, namely that "women are to be referred to in a respectful manner and that includes referring to wives and girlfriends by their given names." The Elder supported this position, and indicated that their behavior was not in keeping with the Native way of dealing with women. There was then a reiteration of the purpose of the group and a commitment to adhere to the rules of the group in order to achieve "change and/or behaviors" towards their partner and others.

The facilitator then re-directed the conversation to the theme of taking personal responsibility for one's own behavior. He also challenged other men in the group to view the concerns voiced in the group from their partner's perspective. The group was reminded that it was important that they be supportive of each other, but that it was more important that they help each other see their "blind spots" in their relationships through confrontation. The Elder was supportive of these concepts and told a traditional story that focused on taking responsibility for their behavior and the need to be frank with each other. The Elder stated at the end of his narrative that "we all have to pull together as a clan, otherwise we can do much harm to each other." Both facilitators encouraged open discussion of these comments, which led to greater cohesion and accountability.

As the weekly sessions progressed, members commented on how the group felt like a family. In this atmosphere of "intimacy," several members were able to share their experiences of being violent with family members and friends. In each instance, members supported each other, while discussing strategies for handling the various situations that arose. The Elder helped the group members to talk about the shame that is brought to the whole First Nations peoples when members of the group are violent with family members. Throughout these sessions the men were acknowledged for their brave disclosures, and were encouraged to stay focused on their treatment goals and the efforts they were making to achieve these goals.

Following significant disclosures of violence against their partners, several members missed one or two of the following sessions. The facilitator then initiated discussion of the impact of the disclosures on the members and the need to put distance between their acts of violence and their partners. By acknowledging their individual responsibility for their violence, a significant step was taken towards reducing violence towards others.

After eight sessions, members were actively challenging each other with regards to their use of violence as a way of resolving difficulties with other family members. Moreover, members were no longer defensive when challenged about their behaviors. Members sought the opinions of each other about the various potentially violent situations they were likely to encounter.

Through the members' open questioning and challenging of each other, the Elder was able to assist them in exploring intergenerational themes within their respective families. In several instances, many members acknowledged becoming aware that they had valuable role models and strengths within their family to draw upon in developing new ways of relating to their partners.

As the group approached the last week of its time together, many men began to talk about what they would do with their Monday nights. Participants made plans for the final session that would involve a "sweat lodge." One participant reported that he was not sure if he could attend the last session. This caused a few men to react negatively, and the issue of separation and the feelings that it evoked were discussed and normalized.

On the final session a late-night sweat lodge was arranged. Before the sweat lodge began, men gathered around the fire and each man spontaneously shared an incident from the group sessions that was meaningful to him. There was much levity and ease among the men. During the sweat lodge, themes related to relationships, self-control and respect for loved ones were introduced. For many of the men, their personal goals were brought to this spiritual place for review and reflection.

Co-Leadership

The use of a male/female and/or Aboriginal/non-Aboriginal co-leadership team offers special advantages for this group. Member's responses to the female worker provide opportunities for further exploration of their relationships and attitudes towards women. While the female co-leader is not expected to speak for their partners, she may often validate the partner's experience relating to the impact of member's beliefs and behavior. The presence of an Aboriginal co-leader provides a concrete and immediate reinforcement of accepted Aboriginal behaviors in a healthy relationship. This offers some of the members an opportunity to observe and model a relationship where power is shared equally between partners, and where decision making and roles are a product of negotiation.

Evaluation

Evaluation is optimally an ongoing process throughout all group sessions. As noted, workers will have members identify what they have learned or gained from the group experience at the end of each session. As is customary with most groups, summary recordings are made following each session. The 25-item Partner Abuse Scale (Attala, Hudson and McSweeney, 1994) is also administered for evaluative purposes.

Conclusion

The workers consistently keep the group focused on member behavior through assisting members to become clearer and specific about their behavior and goals. The workers, particularly during the early phases, will encourage the instillation of group norms of personal accountability, respect and confrontation as tools for the therapeutic work. These norms are reflected in the norm that encourages members to say things that need to be said without undermining the self-esteem of fellow members. However, socialization of new members is largely achieved through the work of veteran group members. Group workers ask veteran members to explain how the group works and then add any missing details. Worker pacing of group work in an Aboriginal community is generally slower to comparable groups in urban areas. Group sessions routinely exceed two hours in duration. Often the cultural metaphor of historical visiting practices is used to help members acquire a sense of the therapeutic work. Historically, visiting would occur over several days and would foster a climate where participants were able to speak from the heart on a deeply personal level.

Group workers, particularly those who are non-Aboriginal, face special obstacles and challenges in group work practice in Aboriginal communities. They face the obstacle of mistrust arising from a legacy of oppression and betrayal by the dominant society. They must be in tune with a non-oppressive and respectful practice in both the design and delivery of treatment groups in Aboriginal communities. They are also challenged to practice in a way that is consistent with the non-violent and respectful attitudes they hope to engender in their clients.

Note

1. In this essay the terms *Aboriginal* and *First Nations* will be used to describe classes of Native persons in Canada. The term *Aboriginal* is used to describe Native-Canadians generally and includes such groups as First Nations, Métis and Inuit people. First Nations people possess a special fiduciary relationship with the federal government under the *Indian Act*. The term *First Nations* has been adopted to recognize the original inhabitants of Canada, and the special relationship they hold with the federal government through treaties and agreements.

Case Study #5

A Feminist Therapy Group for Women Who Struggle with Bulimia

Christine Tauer-Martin

Eating disorders are an expression of the pain, frustration and confusion regarding women's value and identity within the context of a culture that values the masculine over the feminine. One in ten Canadian women have a form of an eating disorder, with bulimia accounting for 40 percent of all eating disorders (Steiger, 2001). Since 92 percent of those who struggle with eating disorders are women, effective interventions need to reflect women's experiences and realities (Harper-Giuffre and MacKenzie, 1993). A feminist therapy group for women who struggle with bulimia was established to respond to this need.

This women's therapy group met together for sixteen weeks with facilitation provided by two female therapists. The focus of the group was to facilitate awareness of the cultural context of eating disorders and develop strategies that replaced disorderly eating patterns through effective goal setting.

Feminist Theoretical Framework

A socio-cultural perspective forms the basis of a feminist analysis of eating disorders with a recognition that bulimia does not result solely from the problems of an individual woman, but in the culture in which she lives. Obsessive preoccupation with body image and size is perpetuated through cultural values, unrealistic media images of women and socially sanctioned prejudice against obesity. Tremendous pressure exists for women to be thin, which denotes acceptance, beauty and success. When thinness is deified and obesity vilified, women internalize impossible standards to obtain acceptance and worth at substantial personal risk. Women experience a profound sense of powerlessness that the thin cultural norm perpetuates, and which women with eating disorders try to rectify through excessive control of their bodies.

Feminist theorists identify distinct developmental processes for women. Rather than maturation occurring through separation and individuation, feminists theorize that female growth results from mutually empathic connections which occur in and through relationships (Jordan, 1997). Therefore, feminist therapy needs to reflect the importance of establishing and maintaining connection through relationships in its conceptualization of group work and the corresponding interventions (Schiller, 1997). If growth results from mutually empathic relating, then the group setting provides fertile soil for much personal enhancement and restoration as well as group development where the attention focuses on developing meaningful relationships.

Feminist values provide the underpinnings from which therapy operates. Core feminist values include the importance of self-determination, empowerment, recognition that personal is political (underscoring the notion of social context) and equalization of the power differential with those in leadership positions (Brown, 1993; Cammaert and Larsen, 1988). These values form the basis from which the group facilitator functions. Group structure, decision making, relationship building and group facilitation style need to reflect the central tenets of feminism. In the context of empathic sharing and empowerment with the minimization of power differentials, the integration of healing and education result (Friedman, 1993; Schiller, 1997; Tantillo, 1998).

Facing the emotions that disorderly eating hides and uncovering the social context for eating disorders demonstrate the healing and educational processes that occur simultaneously within the feminist framework. Recognition and integration of diversity issues must be incorporated into a feminist group model. Consideration of race, class, culture, marital status, sexual orientation in terms of the resulting perception on body image, sex roles and social expectations needs to be deliberately included in group discussions to ensure an inclusive perspective is maintained (Brown, 1993).

Purpose and Goals

The purpose of the women's therapy group for bulimia was to develop meaningful relationships that facilitated individual and group development within the context of understanding the role the eating disorder played in a woman's life. To this end, the overarching goals of the group were to create supportive connections through authentic relationships and to provide support and validation. The group worked towards increasing self-worth, developing greater awareness and understanding of themselves and the impact of external influences, and finally encouraging an individual and collective sense of empowerment (Brown, 1993; Piran, 1993; Schiller, 1997).

The group members determined the specific goals for the group and established the weekly agenda. The women recorded their personal goals and modified them as required to ensure they accurately reflected the desired changes and how to implement them. Women were encouraged to make their own decisions regarding any changes they wanted to secure, which was not always easy for the facilitators. Respecting an individual's choice to continue disorderly eating patterns was essential to invite self-determination and an increased sense of personal control.

Facilitation

Two female therapists who shared similar feminist views facilitated the group. Prior to the beginning of the group, we discussed our perceptions regarding body image, ideal weight, values pertaining to thinness, prejudices against obesity, issues related to power and control, conflict and self-disclosure. If we were asking women to evaluate their own ideas on these issues, we needed to understand how we understood them and how they influenced us daily.

Co-facilitation provided powerful role modeling of shared power and respect for one another despite differences. Demonstrating a leadership model that differed from the dominant culture demonstrated the values of co-operation and collaboration, which encouraged women to take a more active role in the group and nurtured personal capacity.

Pre-Screening

Women were asked to attend an individual interview prior to the start of the group to discuss the purpose and goals of the group, as well as the therapists' theoretical orientation. Providing this information allowed a woman the opportunity to make a choice regarding her involvement and to be aware of what to expect from the group and the therapists. This re-enforced from the beginning the woman's right to self-determination and demystified the therapeutic process by decreasing the power differential between therapist and client (Lawrence and Dana, 1990; Brown, 1993).

Membership and Composition

Nine women with ages ranging from twenty-one to forty-seven were involved in the treatment group. One woman had been previously hospitalized because of the bulimia, five women had been involved in individual therapy and three women were seeking therapy for the first time. Two women had been extensively involved in athletics. Five women worked full time, while two were students and one woman was a full-time caregiver to her three-year-old son. All nine women completed the sixteen-week group, with average attendance of 93 percent.

Agency Context

The group was held at a feminist community counseling agency as a result of growing requests for service. The agency was supportive of the group's purpose and goals and provided individual counseling for women who requested it when the group ended. Childcare was provided and the meetings were held from 6:30 to 8:30 p.m. after a request from the women to accommodate children's bedtime needs.

Group Stage Development

Using Self-In-Relation theory, Schiller (1997) proposes a model for women's group development that more closely reflects women's experiences and more accurately matches their individual and collective strengths. The five-stage model contains the pre-affiliation and separation stages similar to the traditional group models, but also identifies three other stages: establishing a relational base stage, mutuality and interpersonal empathy stage and the challenge and change stage. The major difference in this model is its recognition of women's pre-existing skills for making connections with others as well as women's greatest challenges–staying empathetically connected through conflict (Schiller, 1997). She suggests that since women often find establishing relationships something that they have had significant experience with, stage theory needs to reflect this idea. Also, before women can successfully engage in conflict, connection needs to be established to ensure the potential for successful resolution of the conflict (Cohen, 1996; Schiller, 1997). Therefore, the conflict stage for women's groups evolves later in the group's development after cohesion has been established (Cohen, 1996; Schiller, 1997).

We found Schiller's model useful as the basis for conceptualizing the development of the women's group we offered. The women searched for commonalties in the early stages of group, while comparing eating patterns and sharing personal histories. As the women explored how they maintained a connection with food and disconnected with others, they engaged in the mutuality and interpersonal empathy stage. As suggested by Schiller, the group did not engage in any active conflict until later in group life; the tenth week. By this time relationships among group members and with the facilitators were well established and the levels of intimate sharing and mutual empathy were quite high. One group member challenged another member regarding the secrecy surrounding her bulimic behavior. Assistance from the facilitators enabled both women to express themselves and listen to the other person's perspective. Defensive reactions gave way to meaningful discussion about fears of being misunderstood, judged or rejected, resulting in a greater feelings of connection among group members. The challenged member reported the following week that she had disclosed her bulimic behavior to her mother, which she had never been able to do before. As the group drew to an end, members expressed significant sadness and feelings of loss. Much interest in maintaining relationships was identified and individual members made plans to that end.

Treatment Issues

Common themes emerged during the course of the group. Discussions regarding body image issues, societal pressures towards thinness, stigmas associated with obesity, personal meaning behind disorderly eating patterns, dieting histories, current eating behaviors, self-esteem and finally the connection between relationship with food and relationships with others provided ample opportunity for personal learning and growth. Education regarding healthy dietary considerations and the social context of eating disorders resulted from requests from the women to learn more about these issues.

Awareness and expression of emotions was a challenge that the women often faced in the group. Experienced in negating or ignoring all together their own emotional well-being, many of the women struggled with attunement to underlying feelings of shame, fear, inadequacy and anger. As mutually empathic connections developed among the women, a safe atmosphere allowed for exploration of these uncomfortable emotions. Individual and group goals were assessed on a regular basis to ensure accuracy and modified to reflect more specifically the objectives the women desired to attain as their awareness increased.

Evaluation

At the conclusion of the group the women identified a number of indicators that reflected varying degrees of success towards reaching their personal goals. While the rate of change proved diverse among the women, the common indicators of change included: a decreased number of binging and purging episodes within a week, decreased periods of fasting, increased regularity of meals that included food from all four food groups and moderation in exercise. Also, the women identified and expressed emotions, shared for the first time their experiences with disorderly eating patterns with family and friends and articulated how powerful social influences shaped their identity and self-esteem. Evidence of growth within the group was reflected in group members' ability to identify disconnecting behaviors such as withdrawal or sarcasm, and increased meaningful sharing, validation and appropriate confrontation that reflected empathic connection with one another.

Summary

A feminist framework that incorporated a feminist analysis of eating disorders, recognized women's psychological development patterns and its effects on group development, as well as utilized feminist values to direct practice proved to be an effective means of addressing bulimic behaviors in women. As women recognized the cultural context of eating disorders and understood the connection between their eating habits and their isolation from others, they were able to take decisive action through concrete goal setting. By forging powerful connections with other women who shared similar experiences, women were more willing to take risks and change behaviors that they began to recognize as harmful and self-defeating.

Case Study #6

Adult Separation and Divorce Group

Patricia Wybrow-Patterson

his study focuses on the practice issues involved in group work with adults who are in the process of separation and divorce. The social context of separation and divorce has a great influence upon how people live through its effects. For example, Western society's inattention to the expressions of grief and loss stemming from separation and divorce is essential for the practitioner to consider when providing group treatment. In addition to thinking about the cultural milieu, the practitioner must also understand the process in which the individual development of group members is shaped by a complex matrix of biological, psychological and socio-economic factors (Robbins, Chatterjee and Canda, 1998). Nevertheless, most people who experience separation and divorce pass through similar transition stages. This knowledge helps the practitioner to define group purpose(s) and prepare group goals.

This writer co-facilitated[1] a group designed for both men and women in an agency setting. The group focused on what changes when a relationship ends and what needs to follow so that healing and rebuilding can emerge.

Group Leadership

Two practitioners facilitated this "mixed group" of adults, four men and four women, who share a commonality of their life situation, that is, a recent separation or divorce. Professional readiness consisted of pre-screening activities, prioritizing topics and activities that reflected group goals. The leadership role, absent of leadership struggles, shifted over the eight-week treatment group. The agency decision for co-leadership as a method of practice modeled a consistent mutual respect for each other and demonstrated healthy and constructive conflict resolution.

Group Purpose and Goals

The choice of group work rather than individual counseling reflects the notion that most group experiences are a small microcosm of the larger

---

[1] The terms *co-facilitator* and *co-leader* are used interchangeably.

society. However, unlike the larger society, group rules are built upon respect for other people in the group and the reciprocal development towards problem solving (Travers, 1996). Many of the individuals in the group were unsure about how to identify themselves, how to interact with other people and how to talk about their separation or divorce. Not surprisingly, the group provided an opportunity for members to verbalize, share and "let go" of their terminated relationship. The group also provided practical information to members to help them re-establish a feeling of control, explore the many layers of divorce and examine the stages of separation and divorce. Finally, the group assisted members in the development of a variety of coping strategies to manage feelings of rejection, guilt, shame, anger, denial, and fear, based on issues such as family norms, religion, social status and culture.

This group approach was conceptualized according to the theory of the psycho-educational model and incorporated the fundamental methodology of mutual aid, which encourages group members to share their collective experiences in coping with a stressful event. Sharing personal stories through participation in a group with other people in the same life situation is a significant means to decreasing isolation, gaining new ways of thinking and forming new relationships as resources and supports.

Reflecting social group work method, the goals of this group were numerous, speaking to a blend of the personal and social needs of group members. The group experience innately fulfilled the primary goal of reducing feelings of isolation and alienation.

Feeling out of control is common when a significant relationship dissolves because of separation or divorce. Women, for the most part, are at risk of feeling helpless. A group can provide the opportunity and support to examine enduring feelings of grief and loss and to discuss family of origin patterns that specifically relate to loss, divorce and differentiation of self. Initiation of grieving can reduce anxiety and increase group members' coping.

Other goals were focused on recognizing cognitive and emotional understandings of self as socially constructed concepts reciprocally connected with the larger social structures to assist members with renegotiating and modifying a sense of self and social identity. Members were encouraged to shift their focus from the other and to refocus on themselves. Members gained understanding for personal emotional responsibility, and were encouraged to define themselves as differentiated persons. Group members regained a sense of wholeness, letting go of the "we" identity and shifting to an "I" identity.

Selection

Practitioners generally have a decision to make concerning whether to have a group of only males, only females, or mix the group. Practitioners also need to make a decision as to whether group members consist of adults who have made the decision to end a relationship, adults who have not wanted to end a relationship, or a mix of both. The best combination seems to be one in which groups are diverse and heterogeneous. Diversity and heterogeneity have a great influence upon the effectiveness in group interaction and personal insight and growth (Shulman, 1996).

With that said, necessary criteria to consider for this group to be effective is the balance of variables, such as gender, emotional maturity, age, sexual orientation, culture, race and experience. Consideration of these factors is of utmost importance to prevent the possibility of having an isolate, a scapegoat, or caretaker.

Group Process

The group model approach used combined topic areas with activities and exercises chosen by the co-facilitators. Structured weekly "themes" were utilized to encourage higher member participation and discussion. Check-ins at the beginning of sessions allowed group members to re-connect and share important events that had happened during the week. Check-outs at the end of session offered an opportunity for the group to discuss the impact of the session, review group process and set the tone for the upcoming week.

The first session provided group members with an opportunity to clarify group rules, such as the restriction of sexual relationships with group members until after group ended to inhibit challenging group dynamics. During the first session, group members were asked to introduce themselves and invited to share an "epitaph" statement in memory of their relationship. In so doing, members expressed personal goals and indicators, such as degree of denial or acceptance and degree of anger that might challenge goal realization. The co-facilitators also shared their separation and divorce stories, emphasizing the struggles they shared with other group members and the challenges of re-establishing a sense of wholeness and meaning. By talking in the group, the group members received validation and acceptance from other members and began to feel more connected. The sharing of individual stories indicated a number of common themes and experiences that mirrored weekly themes and topics chosen for sessions. Members found this activity enlightening, specifically because of the common themes of guilt and shame shared among members who made the decision to end a relationship and members who did not want to end a relationship. Some of the members reacted with tears and anger, expressing they felt they had wasted much of their lives. This formative stage of group development is essential to reduce feelings of isolation, stigma and silence.

The third and fourth sessions of the group were focused on "letting go" of the relationship. Members were invited to explore what the partner provided to the meaning of self that is now not there. During this stage, members were encouraged to participate in a ritual exercise. The exercise consisted of selecting an object that represented their relationship, sharing with group members why they selected this particular object, and giving up their attachment to the object, at least in an illusory way, by leaving it behind at the agency after session. Members found this activity quite difficult and stressful, but agreed it was extremely important to participate.

At the end of the fourth session, members reflected on future topics for the remainder of the group. The topics were consistent with the original themes with the addition of sexuality as a topic. Discussions about religion, cultural ties, re-marriage and step-parenting also came up unexpectedly throughout the group sessions. The topics of family of origin influences and self-worth used the group members' individual life histories to examine their beliefs around loss, marriage, divorce and roles. Not only were the "messages" very negative with respect to separation and divorce, but almost all members expressed that marriage was of key value. The group members reviewed whether these messages were consistent with their understanding of themselves or other separated or divorced people that they knew.

At this point a comment needs to be made with respect to the overall emotional tone of the group. Both men and women experienced "up and down" mood swings, described as "being on an emotional roller coaster." The group itself was able to normalize this alternating pattern of vulnerability and strength. In so doing, they were able to examine their beliefs about themselves, their relationships and redefine new meanings. In addition, the group members identified strengths to build upon and to utilize as coping strategies. The session on sexuality was more self-conscious and awkward because of the "mixed" gender group composition.

From the fourth session onward, members brought in books and other resources for other group members' perusal. By the eighth session, most group members had chosen to become socially active together, such as going to movies, coffee, and so forth. Group format evolved from a psycho-educational group to operate as a mutual aid group. The group was prepared for separation throughout the sessions. However, with the successful evolution of the group to a mutual aid format, personal separation losses were minimized considerably.

Measuring Outcomes

In terms of when to measure and what, it was determined that evaluation needs to be an ongoing process, beginning at the pre-screening stage. Concrete measurement of indicators can be identified as characteristics of empowerment. Some of these might include: acceptance of separation or divorce, emotional and cognitive adjustment to separation and divorce, decreased feelings of shame, guilt and isolation, ability to develop and maintain relationships, satisfaction with relationships and ability to develop a differentiated sense of self.

It is important to note that complex life circumstances, such as second or third divorces, multi-cultural or biracial family forms and so on, may require unique criteria in group treatment approaches.

Conclusion

This study has dealt primarily with adult experience of separation and divorce and the importance of attention to grief work, release and redefinition of a whole self, particularly in the efforts to overcome the invisible and visible societal obstacles that impact on people's lived experiences. The group treatment approach has to do with meeting the specific needs of the separating and divorcing members, while at the same time facilitating movement through the attachment-detachment cycle. The separation and divorce process is a long-term process that is more often than not painful and debilitating. It is a challenging process, which involves a range of intense emotions and significant decisions. The intent of this study is not to suggest that adult separation and divorce treatment groups are easy, growthful, and members readily achieve adjustment to life situations. Rather, my intent is to stress that separation and divorce can be a corrective leading to higher levels of personal functioning, and with participation in group treatment, the painful work of deconstructing and reconstructing an identity and understanding its social context can have a breadth of long-range outcomes.

EVALUATION IN SOCIAL GROUP TREATMENT

Evaluation in social group treatment is a diverse and complex process, yet it is an essential component of all group treatment. Prior to the beginning of the first session, it is important for the worker to have a clear plan for the evaluation of the many aspects of group treatment. This plan includes establishing, articulating and documenting clear individual, worker, group and agency goals and objectives for treatment. Even when the goals are outlined, there are other aspects of the treatment process that require measurement and evaluation. The effectiveness of the worker's or workers' interventions, the impact and appropriateness of the program content on members and the individual's affective, cognitive and behavioral growth are only a few of the many variables to be measured and evaluated. There is also a need to examine the impact of the worker's subjective responses to the treatment process.

SECTION 4: CONTENTS

11

Evaluation of Group Treatment

E valuation is a professional responsibility in all forms of treatment practice. Planning for evaluation of the many components of group treatment will encourage the worker to ensure that there is as much specificity about these components as is possible.

The complex process of evaluation cannot be carried on in a vacuum but must be done within the context of the sponsoring organization, the referral source (if one is involved), the environment, the client, the worker and the group. Each sponsoring organization determines its goals and objectives for the client groups it plans to serve. The criteria outlined by Trecker (1972) for the evaluation of social group work in an agency setting are equally applicable to organizations that sponsor treatment services. These criteria are: purpose, community setting, constituency, program, the board, administrative personnel, professional personnel, volunteer personnel, facilities, financial resources and practices, relationship with national organizations, community and public relations, reporting and appraisal, relationship with central planning bodies and long-range planning (pp. 203–207).

In planning with and for the group the worker should clearly document the specific individual and group areas targeted for change. In addition, the specific criteria that will be used to determine that change has occurred should be articulated. Both clients and worker may be involved in recording evidence of changed behaviors, affect and thinking. In a group for mothers experiencing disciplinary problems with their children, for example, the worker and the group identified problem areas such as open defiance by their children and frequent temper tantrums. The mothers outlined the specific kinds of behaviors that occurred and when they occurred. Moreover, they identified the cause of their children's behavior as in some way connected to the manner in which they were reprimanding their children. The group helped each other to plan strategies for reprimanding their children differently and devised ways of measuring the changes that occurred in their children's behavior and how mothers felt after each reprimand. This would help the mothers to recognize how changes in their behavior influenced their children's behavior. It may also help them to understand how their behavior could reflect intangibles, such as a poor self image.

The foregoing implies that the expected client change can be stated in specific terms that may then be observable and measurable. The goals and objectives for each client and for the group should be as concrete as possible. For example, the client's expectations of the group treatment process may be to develop a better self image. As stated, such a goal is not quantifiable. At this early stage of the treatment process, the worker may intervene in such a manner as to help a client to operationalize the behaviors, feelings and thoughts to be changed. The data resulting from these operationalized goals can then be observed, measured and analyzed by the worker.

Similarly, the group's goals and processes, the interventions of the worker and their effectiveness can be articulated in specific terms that can be measured and analyzed. Many of the evaluative criteria outlined by Trecker (1972) regarding social group work readily apply to social group work treatment. These criteria are in no way definitive but serve as a stimulus for all professionals working with treatment groups.

Evaluative criteria for group work should take into account the several phases of the group work as a whole. Inasmuch as social group work involves individuals, groups, workers and agencies, it is necessary to see what good group work practice calls for in the way of specific behavior of each.

Effective group work depends largely upon what happens in the group itself. Good group work results:

(1) when the members of the group propose, plan, carry out, and evaluate their own program experiences with the assistance of the group worker;

(2) when the members of the group enjoy status and a relationship of mutual acceptance that makes for social adjustment—evidence of this status and acceptance appears in the interactions and relationships among the members of the group;

(3) when a group works together cooperatively and democratically with a wide range of participation if possible, every member participating to the extent of his ability;

(4) when the behavior of the group is such that it accepts help, guidance and counsel from the group worker and other resource persons in the agency and community;

(5) when a group develops not only consciousness of its own self but also wholesome relationships with other groups in the agency and the community; and

(6) when the group shows evidence of a developing social consciousness that enables it to take responsibility for leadership in vital af-
fairs of the community (p. 213).

Additional criteria of good group work can be formulated in terms of
worker behavior. Actually, the way in which the worker carries out his responsibilities, influences the extent to which the group can be a positive
resource for individual growth and change.

Recording

Recording is essential in the evaluative process. Since there are many elements, interactions, and changes over time to be evaluated in group
treatment, workers cannot expect to hold this information only in their
memories. Records provide permanent accounts of the process, interactions, goals, objectives and outcomes of the treatment process. Fisher and
Bloom make the point that the whole process of recording should be built
into the procedural guidelines that the worker ordinarily uses as he or she
collects and assumes various sources of information about the client/sys-
tem problem situation before beginning intervention. Recording is an
integral part of practice (p. 75).

Recording should therefore be systematically ordered and consistently
reflect organizational, worker, client and group rules and procedures in
specific terms. In addition, items regarding worker effectiveness, effort and
performance should be documented along with the effectiveness of the client's contribution, participation and measures of affective, cognitive and
behavioral changes as clients move toward the achievement of their goals.
Recording, whether audio, visual or written, lends itself to scrutiny and
analysis. It must be acknowledged, however, that much of the data workers
collect and record must be considered "soft" in a scientific sense. Nevertheless, these data should be recorded in an organized manner.

According to Lindsay (cited in Trecker, 1972), there are five basic principles of recording: flexibility, selection, readability, confidentiality and
worker acceptance. To these we would add a sixth—recording. If such elements are incorporated into all group recording, then the worker will be
able to analyze and order the data in such a way as to evaluate:

- the group's movement through its stages of development;
- the factors that facilitated or hindered group cohesion;
- the effect of the group on the achievement of individual
  goals;
- the goal attainment of worker, individual and group; and
- worker effectiveness.

The primary purpose of recording is to enhance the quality and effectiveness of the services provided to the client. Admittedly, this task is not easy and there are no clear guidelines. Garvin (1981), in *Contemporary Group Work*, acknowledges the difficulties inherent in evaluating group work practice, yet encourages the workers to be cognizant of existing knowledge and technologies relevant to evaluation. The argument is made, justifiably, that the worker has an obligation to the group members. They have a right to examine whether or not their investment in the group work process has attained the goals they have established for themselves. Furthermore, workers must know which of the procedures they employ to facilitate individual change are the most effective and efficient (p. 186).

Supervision

Built into the evaluation of group treatment is a component of supervision. The worker must provide information about the group so that the group and the worker's performance in the group can be evaluated. The supervisory process requires the selective recording of events, impressions, judgments, and opinions of what occurs in treatment. The purpose of supervision is to improve the quality of service to clients in keeping with the goals and objectives of the organization under whose auspices the treatment services are offered. Summary records must be kept to facilitate supervision.

These summaries help the worker to think through what is occurring in the group and at the same time provides the supervisor with some understanding of the treatment situation from the worker's perspective. These records are likely to reflect the areas of competence and the difficulties faced by the worker. Again, records may be visual, audio or written. The visual and audio forms cover much that occurs in face-to-face sessions. The written form has to be more selective and may be organized around one or two events that occur in the group at the beginning, during the work or middle phase and during the ending, and how these events were handled. It is useful to include diagnostic statements that reflect on the status of group development, and the direction of treatment and evidence of changes occurring. In addition, the worker's subjective responses to the events and situations should be identified.

Records should be reviewed by the supervisor and the worker prior to a supervisory session so that the items to be discussed may be selected. These discussions would explore with the worker what is occurring in the group and examine treatment alternatives. This process would also validate the worker's successes. It is well known in helping professions that a good supervisory relationship has a parallel process in the relationship that develops between the worker and the client. If there is an honest, open and trusting relationship between the worker and supervisor, it is likely that the same type of relationship will exist between the worker and the client. Workers tend to model their behaviors on those of their supervisors.

Developing and keeping records are critical in group treatment. Trecker (1972) observes that, in fact, it is doubtful whether evaluations of program, individual growth or worker performance can be satisfactorily made without records. Although partial judgments can be made on the basis of memory, thorough evaluation is possible only if adequate records have been kept (p. 220).

Transference and Counter-Transference

Throughout this text we have referred to the worker's subjective responses or the use of self in treatment. Embodied in these phrases are the well-documented concepts of transference and counter-transference. Corey and Corey's (1982) explanation of these terms coincides with our understanding of them:

> transference consists of the feelings that clients project onto the therapist. These feelings usually have to do with relationships the clients have experienced in the past, and, when they are attributed to the therapist, they are not realistic. Counter-transference refers to the feelings that are aroused in the therapist by clients; feelings that, again, have more to do with unresolved conflict in a past relationship than with any feature of the present relationship (p. 135).

Throughout the group treatment process, issues related to the subjective responses of both worker and client arise. Through peer consultation, supervision and reflection, workers may become more sensitive to such issues. In fact, part of the evaluative process in group treatment is an examination of how the worker deals with the client's subjective responses and his own. These feelings should be identified whenever possible and used to facilitate individual and group change during the treatment process. If these feelings are not acknowledged and dealt with, the worker or the client may unwittingly sabotage the group treatment process. The assigning of a significant role to another can provide opportunities for both client and worker to gain insight, to learn and to change. For example, in a group of inmates in a reformatory, Tom made the following comment to the worker: *You are as controlling as my father.* To this the worker replied: *Let us examine together our behaviors so that we may understand why you feel the way you do.* Through this exploration all members may learn something about themselves and their responses to others.

SECTION 4: SUGGESTED READINGS

- Bernard, H.S., and Drob, S. (1985). The experience of patients in conjoint individual and group psychotherapy. *International Journal of Group Psychotherapy, 35*, 129–146.
- Bernstein, S. (Ed.). (1965). *Explorations in Social Group Work.* Boston: Boston University, School of Social Work.
- Bradford, L.P. (Ed.). (1978). *Group Development (2nd ed.).* La Jolla, California: University Associates.
- Cox, M. (1973). The group therapy interaction chronogram. *British Journal of Social Work, 3*, 243–256.
- Flapan, D., and Fenchel, G.H. (1984). Countertransference in group psychotherapy. *Group, 8(3),* 17–29.
- Fogelman, E., and Savran, B. (1980). Brief group therapy with offspring of holocaust survivors: Leaders' reactions. *American Journal of Orthopsychiatry, 50*, 96–108.
- Garland, J.A., Jones, H.E., and Kolodny, R.L. (1965). A model for stages of development in social work groups. In S. Bernstein, S. (Ed.). *Explorations in Social Group Work.* Boston: Boston University School of Social Work.
- Hannah, S. (1984). Countertransference in-patient group psychotherapy: Implications for technique. *International Journal of Group Psychotherapy, 34(2),* 257–272.
- Husband, D., and Scheunemann, J.R. (1972). The use of group process in teaching termination. *Child Welfare, 51*, 505–513.
- *Journal of Research on Social Work Practice* (1991). Volume 1. Newbury Park, California: Sage Periodicals Press.
- Kahn, E.M. (1979). The parallel process in social work treatment and supervision. *Social Casework, 60*, 520–528.
- Lesser, I.M., and Godofsky, I.D. (1983). Group treatment for chronic patients: Educational and supervisory aspects. *International Journal of Group Psychotherapy, 33*, 535–546.
- Munson, C. (1981). Symbolic interaction theory for small group treatment. *Social Casework, 60*, 167–174.
- Schwartz, W., and Zalba, S. (1975). *The Practice of Group Work.* New York: Columbia University Press.
- Weiner, M.F. (1983). The assessment and resolution of impasse in group psychotherapy. *International Journal of Group Psychotherapy, 33*, 313–331.

Conclusion

hroughout this text, the many ways that theory informs practice in group treatment have been highlighted. The use of theory is the distinguishing hallmark between professional helping and lay helping. Professional helping must be focused, goal-oriented, and logical and sequential in thinking and application. Theory helps the professional to do that. Theory provides the professional with a way of conceptualizing the treatment process. It helps the professional to plan, implement and evaluate treatment in an orderly manner. At the same time, it helps the practitioner to gain some objectivity around identifying the problem, drawing out the data in relation to the problem, assessing that data, examining alternatives, and helping the client to focus on an alternative with attending consequences and to make choices in relation to their situation.

The use of theory, then, helps the practitioner to provide a more effective service to clients. Theory will suggest strategies in the treatment process, how clients can be expected to behave, how various interventions are likely to affect the client as an individual and the group as a whole, and, at the same time, helps to structure how evaluation will occur throughout the group treatment sequence. Actually, evaluation is only possible if there is a theoretical perspective from which to draw. Theory helps in the understanding of group treatment options. It also indicates what can be expected from a particular client group, and what kinds of treatment approaches would be helpful in reaching the goals and objectives of the organization, the client system and the worker.

There is no suggestion in our comments that theory should be followed slavishly. Doing so does not necessarily ensure success. Theory serves as a guide to practice. It is also true that from practice theories are modified and, in fact, theories are often developed from practice realities. There is then movement, so theory does inform practice and at the same time practice influences on theory. Since practice affects theory, theory is constantly changing to reflect changing environments, changing clients and changing technologies in terms of helping.

Practitioners have two primary responsibilities in relation to theory and practice. These are, first, to ensure that they are up-to-date with existing theory and that they allow that theory to guide and direct practice. At the same time, the second responsibility is to structure practice in such a manner that the data and experience gained from practice helps the worker change his or her theoretical orientations. Neither theory nor practice are static entities. They constantly interact with each other through the practitioners and are reflected in more effective and efficient group treatment service to clients.

The criteria for evaluating the other aspects of social group treatment are numerous and very varied. Changes that occur within the group and with members, including the worker, are difficult to measure at the best of times. In fact, many of the variables observed in small groups do not readily lend themselves to measurement. But difficulties should not deter the worker from identifying hypotheses as they relate to group treatment practice. The general goal of group treatment is to effect individual changes in affect, cognition and behavior. Therefore, the worker should plan or design strategies for measuring changes in client functioning and in how intervention practices affect the change process of the client as an individual and as part of the collectivity—the group.

Effective practice assumes effective evaluation. If the practitioner has as a major goal learning how to develop the skill of setting and achieving goals for group treatment, then the critical evaluation of practice is required. It is only as the practitioner mirrors the skills of setting and achieving goals that the client will be able to learn and develop his or her capacities for setting and achieving goals in relation to expressed and/or felt needs.

The practitioner must therefore use existing theory to critically evaluate practice and sequentially critique theory in the context of current practice. As these processes become part and parcel of group treatment for the practitioner, the client and the agency, all involved are likely to develop the skills and capacities to manage their personal and professional lives in more satisfying and creative ways than before group treatment began.

Through group treatment all parties are beginning an ever-ascending spiral for personal and professional growth that ideally becomes more integrated between achievement and reflection. The apex of the spiral may never be achieved, but client and worker may have learned ways of enhancing their human functioning for their individual benefit and that of the society at large.

Bibliography

- Alissi, A.A. (Ed.). (1980). *Perspectives on Social Group Work Practice*. New York: The Free Press.
- Attala J., Hudson W., and McSweeney, M. (1994). A partial validation of two short-form partner abuse scales. *Women and Health, 21(2/3)*, 125–139.
- Barnes, G.G. (1975). Deprived adolescents: A use for group work. *British Journal of Social Work, 5*, 149–160.
- Bennis, W.G., Benne, K.D., Chin R., and Corey K.E. (Eds.). (1976). *The Planning of Change (3rd ed.)*. New York: Holt, Rinehart and Winston.
- Bernard, H.S., and Drob, S. (1985). The experience of patients in conjoint individual and group psychotherapy. *International Journal of Group Psychotherapy, 35*, 129–146.
- Bernstein, S. (Ed.). (1965). *Explorations in Social Group Work*. Boston: Boston University School of Social Work.
- Bradford, L.P. (Ed.) (1978). *Group Development (2nd. ed.)*. La Jolla, California: University Associates.
- Brandler, S., and Roman C.P. (1991). *Group Work. Skills and Strategies for Effective Interventions*. New York: Haworth Press.
- Briere, J., Evans, D., Runtz M., and Wall, T. (1988) Symptomology in men who were molested as children: A comparison study. *American Journal of Orthopsychiatry, 58(3)*, 457–461.Bruckner, D., and Johnson, P. (1987). Treatment for adult male victims of childhood sexual
- Bruckner, D., and Johnson, P. (1987). Treatment for adult male victims of childhod sexual abuse. *Social Casework, 68(2)*, 81–87.
- Budman, S.H., Bennet, M.J., and Wisneski, M.J. (1980). Short-term group psychotherapy: An adult developmental model. *International Journal of Group Psychotherapy, 30*, 63–75.
- Carbino, R. (1982). Group work with natural parents in permanency planning. *Social Work with Groups, 5(4)*, 7–30.
- Compton, B., and Galaway, B. (1984). *Social Work Processes (3rd ed.)*. Illinois: The Dorsey Press.
- Corey, G., and Corey, M.S. (1982). *Groups: Process and Practice (2nd ed.)*. Monterey, California: Brooks/Cole Publishing Co.
- Corey, G., Corey, M.S., Callanan, P.J., and Russell, J.M. (1982). *Group Techniques*. Monterey, California: Brooks/Cole Publishing Co.
- Cox, M. (1973). The group therapy interaction chronogram. *British Journal of Social Work, 3*, 243–256.
- Currie, David W. (1983). A Toronto Model. *Social-Work-with-Groups, 6(3/4)*, 179–188.
- Davis, F.B., and Lohr, N.E. (1971). Special problems with the use of cotherapists in group psychotherapy. *International Journal of Group Psychotherapy, 21*, 143–158.
- Dimock, H. (1976). *Planning Group Development*. Montreal: Concordia University.
- Dobash, R.E., and Dobash, R.P. (1992). The therapeutic society. In *Women, Violence, and Social Change*. (pp. 242–250). London and New York: Rutledge.

- Empey, L.J. (1977). Clinical group work with multi-handicapped adolescents. *Social Casework, 58*, 593–599.

- Epstein, N. (1976). Techniques of brief therapy with children and parents. *Social Casework, 57*, 317–323.

- Fisher, J., and Bloom, M. (1982). *Evaluating Practice: Guidelines for the Accountable Professional.* New Jersey: Prentice-Hall.

- Flapan, D., and Fenchel, G.H. (1984). Countertransference in group psychotherapy. *Group, 8(3)*, 17–29.

- Fogelman, E., and Savran, B. (1980). Brief group therapy with offspring of holocaust survivors: Leaders' reactions. *American Journal of Orthopsychiatry, 50*, 96–108.

- Galinsky, M.J., and Schopler, J.H. (1980). Structuring co-leadership in social work training. *Social Work with Groups,* 3(4), 51–63.

- Garland, J.A., Jones, H.E., and Kolodny, R.L. (1965). A model for stages of development in social work groups. In S. Bernstein, (Ed.). *Explorations in Social Group Work.* Boston: Boston University School of Social Work.

- Garland, J., and West, J. (1964). Differential assessment and treatment of the school age child: Three group approaches. *Social Work with Groups, 7(4)*, 57–70.

- Garvin, C.D. (1981). *Contemporary Group Work.* New Jersey: Prentice-Hall, Inc.

- Garvin, C.D. (1984). The changing contexts of social group work practice: Challenge and opportunity. *Social Work with Groups, 7(1)*, 3–19.

- Getzel, G. (1982). Group work with kin and friends caring for the elderly. *Social Work with Groups, 5(4)*, 91–102.

- Gitterman, A., and Shulman, L. (Eds.) (1986). *Mutual Aid Groups and the Life Cycle.* Itasca, Illinois: F.E. Peacock Publishers.

- Glassman, U., and Kates, L. (1983). Authority themes and worker-group transactions: Additional dimensions to the stages of group development. *Social Work with Groups, 6(2)*, 33–52.

- Glassman U., and Kates L. (1990). *Group Work. A Humanistic Approach.* Newbury Park, California: Sage Publications.

- Golden, N., Chirlin, P., and Shone, B. (1979). Tuesday children. *Social Casework, 51*, 599–605.

- Goodman, K., and Rothman, B. (1984). Group work in infertility treatment. *Social Work with Groups,* 7(1), 79–97.

- Gordy, P. (1983). Group work that supports adult victims of childhood incest. *Social Casework, 64*, 300–307.

- Hannah, S. (1984). Countertransference in-patient group psychotherapy: Implications for technique. *International Journal of Group Psychotherapy, 34(2)*, 257–272.

- Hart, M. (1996). Sharing circles: Utilizing traditional practice methods for teaching, helping and supporting. In S. O'Meara and D. West (Eds.). *From our eyes: Learning from indigenous peoples.* Toronto: Garamond Press.

- Hartford, M.E., and Parsons, R. (1982). Uses of groups with relatives of dependent older adults. *Social Work with Groups, 5(2)*, 77–90.

- Heap, K. (1984). Purposes in social work with groups: Their interrelatedness with values and methods: A historical and prospective view. *Social Work with Groups, 7(1)*, 21–54.

- Holman, S.L. (1985). A group program for borderline mothers and their toddlers. *International Journal of Group Psychotherapy, 35*, 79–93.

- Hurley, D.J. (1974). Resistance and work in adolescent groups, *Social Work With Groups, 7(4)*, 71–81.

- Husband, D., and Scheunemann, J.R. (1972). The use of group process in teaching termination. *Child Welfare, 51*, 505–513.

- (2001). *International Journal of Group Psychotherapy, 51(1)*. Special Issue on Group Therapy and Substance Abuse, *51(1)*.

- Kahn, E.M. (1979). The parallel process in social work treatment and supervision. *Social Casework, 60*, 520–528.

- Kell, B.L., and Mueller, W.J. (1966). *Impact and Change: A Study of Counseling Relationships*. New Jersey: Prentice-Hall Inc.

- Klein, A.G. (1972). *Effective Group Work*. New York: Association Press.

- Korda, Lois J., and Pancrazio, James J. (1989). Limiting negative outcome in group practice. *Journal-for-Specialists-in-Group-Work, 14(2)*, 112–120.

- Lee, J.A., and Park, D.N. (1978). A group approach to the depressed adolescent girl in foster care. *American Journal of Orthopsychiatry, 48(3)*, 516–527.

- Lesser, I.M., and Godofsky, I.D. (1983). Group treatment for chronic patients: Educational and supervisory aspects. *International Journal of Group Psychotherapy, 33*, 535–546.

- Levine, B. (1965). Principles for developing an ego supportive group treatment service. *Journal of Social Service Review, 39*.

- Levine, B. (1980). Co-leadership approaches to learning group work. *Social Work with Groups, 3(4)*, 35–38.

- Lewis, Karen G. (1989). Teaching gender issues to male/female group therapists. *Journal of Independent Social Work, 3(4)*, 125–139.

- Lowy, L. (1982). Social group work with vulnerable older persons: A theoretical perspective. *Social Work With Groups, 5(2)*, 21–32.

- Lundin, W., and Anonov, B. (1952). The use of co-therapists in group psychotherapy. *Journal of Consulting Psycholog, 16*, 76–80.

- MacLennan, B.W. (1965). Co-therapy. *International Journal of Group Psychotherapy, 15*, 154–165.

- McGee, T.F., and Schuman, B.N., (1970). The nature of the co-therapy relationship. *International Journal of Group Psychotherapy, 20*, 25–35.

- Monane, J.H. (1967). *A Sociology of Human Systems*. New York: Appleton Century Crofts.

- Morrissette, V., McKenzie, B., and Morrissette, L. (1993). Towards an Aboriginal model of social work practices. *Canadian Social Work Review, 10(1)*, 91–108.

- Moyer, S. (1992). Race, gender, and homicide: Comparisons between aboriginals and other Canadians. *Canadian Journal of Criminology*, 387–402.

- Munson, C. (1981). Symbolic interaction theory for small group treatment. *Social Casework, 60*, 167–174.

- Myers, K. (1996). *An Overview of Corrections Research and Development Projects on Family Violence*. (March). Public Works and Government Services Canada.

- Nobler, H. (1980). A peer group for therapists: Successful experience in sharing. *International Journal of Group Psychotherapy, 30(1)*, 51–62.

- O'Meara, S. and West, D. (Eds.). (1996). *From our eyes: Learning from indigenous peoples*. (pp. 59–73). Toronto: Garamond Press.

- Ormont, L.R. (1984). The leader's role in dealing with aggression in groups. *International Journal of Group Psychotherapy, 34*, 553–572.

- Pfeifer, G.D., and Weinstock-Savoy, D. (1984). Peer culture and the organization of self and object representations in children's psychotherapy groups. *Social Work With Groups, 7(4)*, 39–56.

- Reid, K.E. (1977). Worker authenticity in group work. *Clinical Journal of Social Work, 5*, 3–16.

- Robbins, S., Chatterjee, P, and Canda, E. (1998). Theories of life span development. In Robbins, S., Chatterjee, P., and Canda, E. (Eds.). *Contemporary human behavior theory: A critical perspective for social work*. (pp.188–230). Toronto, Ont.: Allyn & Bacon.

- Ross, A.L., and Bernstein, N.D. (1976). A framework for the therapeutic use of group activities. *Child Welfare, 55(9)*, 627–640.
- Scharlach, A.E. (1985). Social group work with institutionalized elders: A task centered approach. *Social Work With Groups, 8(3)*.
- Schwartz, W., and Zalba, S. (1975). *The Practice of Group Work*. New York: Columbia University Press.
- Sebold, J. (1987). Indicators of child sexual abuse in males. *Social Casework, 68(2)*, 75-80.
- Shulman, L. (1968). *A Casebook of Social Work with Groups: The Meditating Model*. New York: Council on Social Work Education.
- Shulman, L. (1979). *The Skills of Helping Individuals and Groups*. Itasca, Illinois: Peacock Publishers Inc.
- Shulman, L. (1988). *Dynamics and Skills for Group Work: An Interactional Approach*. Workshop conducted, Waterloo, Canada.
- Shulman, L. (1996). Social work with groups. In Stempler, B., Glass, M., and Savinelli, C. (Eds.). *Social group work today and tomorrow: Moving from theory to advanced training and practice*. Binghamton, N.Y.: The Haworth Press, Inc.
- Smith, J.D., Walsh, R.J., and Richardson, M.A. (1985). The clown club: A structured fantasy approach to group therapy with the latency-age child. *International Journal of Group Psychotherapy, 35*, 49–64.
- Starak, Y. (1981). Co-leadership: A new look at sharing group work. *Social Work with Groups, 4(¾)*, 145–157.
- Travers, A. (1996). Redefining adult identity. In Stempler, B., Glass, M. and Savinelli, C. (Eds.). *Social group work today and tomorrow: Moving from theory to advanced training and practice*. Binghamton, N.Y.: The Haworth Press, Inc.
- Trecker, H.B. (1972). *Social Group Work: Principles and Practices*. New York: Association Press.
- Vander Mey, B. (1988). The sexual victimization of male children: A review of previous research. *Child Abuse and Neglect, 12*, 61–72.
- Weiner, M.F. (1983). The assessment and resolution of impasse in group psychotherapy. *International Journal of Group Psychotherapy, 33*, 313–331.
- Whitaker, D.W. (1975). Some conditions for effective work with groups. *British Journal of Social Work, 5(4)*, 421–439.
- Winter, S.K. (1976). Developmental stages in the roles and concerns of group co-leaders. *Small Group Behavior, 7*, 349–362.
- Yalom, Irvin, (1985). *The Theory and Practice of Group Psychotherapy*, (3rd ed.). Basic Books, Inc., New York.

Index

acceptance and support, 97

affect, 11, 37, 63-64, 95, 157, 164

affective functioning, 39-40, 44, 52, 63, 70, 78, 85, 87, 91, 98, 100, 155, 159

ambivalence, feelings of, 53, 67, 73, 86, 88-89, 98

anxiety, 18, 43, 45, 53, 61, 63, 65, 71, 73, 78-79, 117

approach-avoidance, 67

attitudes, 13, 19-20, 96, 101

authority, 17, 23-24, 27, 37, 76, 78-79, 81, 83, 88, 91, 95, 119

behavior, 11, 18, 31-32, 34-35, 41, 44, 50, 63-64, 67, 75, 77, 79-81, 87, 89-90, 95-96, 107, 116, 157-159, 164
testing of new, 98

benefits, 52

Brandler and Roman, 113

challenging of members, 99

climate, psycho-social, 13, 21, 23, 56, 61, 63, 97

closed groups, 41-42

co-leadership, 113, 115, 117-118, 120
disadvantages of, 118

co-workers, 45, 114, 117

codes of behavior, 13, 21

cognitive, 39, 52, 70, 91, 98, 100, 155, 159

cohesion, 52, 63, 66, 82, 85, 87, 92-93, 95, 97, 100-101, 106, 159

communications, 13-14, 17-19, 22, 30, 63-64, 69, 76-78, 101, 118

confidentiality, 61, 68-69, 71, 75, 89, 159

conflict, 14-15, 18, 20, 29, 46, 76, 80-81, 88, 90, 101, 107, 114-116, 118-119, 161

contract, 43-44, 61, 70-71, 75-76, 79-81, 83, 86, 91, 98, 103, 106, 109, 111

Corey and Corey, 87, 161

counter-transference, 37, 161

culture, 13, 15, 19, 45

curative factors, 52, 55

decision making, 21, 39

denial, 104, 106

dialoguing, 53, 61, 65-66

differentiation, 60, 95-96, 98-102

doubts, 65

emotional and psychological positions, testing of, 77

evaluation, 22, 34, 39, 41, 108-109, 116, 155, 157, 160-161, 163

exploration and affiliation, 69

family dynamics, re-enactment of, 90

fears, 65

Fisher and Bloom, 159

flight, 104-105

formalizing of relationships, 80

funding, 13, 15-16

Garvin, 160

Glassman and Kates, 49

goals, 13-19, 26, 28-33, 35-37, 40-42, 46, 52-55, 61, 65, 71, 75, 79, 81, 85-87, 89-91, 96-100, 104, 106-109, 113-117, 119, 155, 157-160, 163

group composition, 14, 29, 36, 40, 42-44, 47

group size, 41-42

AGMV Marquis

MEMBER OF SCABRINI MEDIA

Quebec, Canada
2003